FIRST AID
for **YOUR** Health

Edward E. Moody, Jr., Ph.D.

Making 10 Therapeutic Life Changes

randall house

First Aid for Your Health
Making 10 Therapeutic Life Changes

© 2013 by Edward E. Moody Jr.

Published by Randall House
114 Bush Road
Nashville, TN 37217
Visit www.randallhouse.com

13-ISBN 9780892656837

Printed in the United States of America

MAKING 10 THERAPEUTIC LIFE CHANGES

*Beloved, I pray that all may go well with
you and that you may be in good health,
as it goes well with your soul.*

3 John 1:2

Health. We hear about health all the time, from the debate over the Affordable Care Act to the newsstand carrying the latest diet fad. What if you could be healthy (or healthier) by making some slight (albeit critical), changes to your life? In this booklet, we will look at how you can make 10 therapeutic life changes that lead to better health. They are based upon the teachings of Scripture and supported by solid research. They might surprise you.

Why bother?

When it comes to health, there are vastly different approaches. Some people seem to think of nothing else while others appear to have never given their health any thought at all. If you live in the United States, you live at an odd time. Though there have been remarkable advances in medical technology (e.g., knee replacement surgery, organ transplant), we live in the midst of a perfect health storm. The United States is growing greyer everyday as a "silver tsunami" of 10,000 joins the roll of Medicare daily.[1] At the same time, health care costs are climbing. It costs around $15,000 for knee replacement surgery. As the population has aged, the number of knee replacements among Medicare patients has in-

The Impact in the United States

- Heart disease is the leading cause of death (accounting for 35% of all deaths), around 7.6% of the population suffer from coronary heart disease, and 82% of people who die from coronary heart disease are 65 or older.

- Cancer is the second leading cause of death, accounting for 25% of all deaths.[2] Cancer is the leading cause of death for women aged 40 to 79 years, and men aged 60 to 79 years. The lifetime probability of being diagnosed with cancer is 45% for men and 38% for women. The most common types of cancer are lung, breast, and colon in women, and lung, prostate, and colon in men.[3]

- Stroke is the third leading cause of death, afflicting nearly seven million Americans. This affects 2.7% of men and 2.5% of women. States with the highest stroke rates are Arkansas, Oklahoma, South Carolina, North Carolina, and Oregon.[4]

creased from 93,230 in 1990 to 243,802 in 2010. It is estimated the number could be as high as 3.48 million a year by 2030.[5] As costs grow, the nation is becoming unable to meet them. In 1965, 81 million workers paid for the benefits of 20 million retirees, resulting in a 4 to 1 worker-retiree ratio. Today, the ratio has fallen to 2.8 to 1, and the ratio is expected to drop to 2 to 1 by 2035. The country's birth rate has fallen to 63.2 per 1,000 women of childbearing age, the lowest at any point since the nation began keeping records in 1920. Therefore, the prospects for viable Medicare and Social Security programs are dimming. At this rate Medicare will be exhausted in 2024.[6]

The financial problem is further complicated by a lack of services. The country is also beginning to feel the impact of a physician shortage. There are currently 15,230 fewer primary

The Cost in the US

- Cardiovascular diseases cost $403 billion per year.[7]

- The impact of strokes cost $70 billion per year[8], and is the leading cause of long-term disability.[9]

care physicians than the Department of Health and Human Services estimate the US needs. The Association of American Medical Colleges estimates that by 2025 the shortage (including specialists) will climb to 130,000.[10] It is unlikely there will be enough physicians or acute care facilities for the aging population that will need them in the future.[11] Therefore, it is critical to do what we can to take control of our own health.

Unhealthy Population

> The years of our life are seventy, or even by reason of strength eighty; yet their span is but toil and trouble; they are soon gone, and we fly away.
>
> Psalm 90:10

All of this is happening at a time when the US population has become increasingly unhealthy. The average life expectancy at birth in the US is 78.7 years of age (81.1 for women and 76.3 for men).[12] However, many fear that today's children will have a shorter life expectancy. The obesity rate continues to climb. Currently 13.4% of the US population are obese (anywhere from 5 to 17% of children).[13]

The health care costs for obese individuals are about twice that of normal weight individuals.[14] The impact is already being felt with the spike in strokes in young people. According to the American Stroke Association, in the last 12 years there has been a 51% increase in hospitalization due to stroke for men ages 15 through 34, and a 17% increase for women that age.[15] To further cloud the picture, 30% of the adult population aged 18 or older have hypertension or high blood pressure[16] placing them at risk for heart disease, and increasing their risk for stroke by 3 to 5 times.[17] Hypertension is known as the "silent killer." It causes the heart muscle to thicken and become stiff, damaging the inside lining of the coronary arteries and increases the likelihood that fatty deposits will form in them, ultimately causing the arteries to narrow and close up.

> Hypertension is defined as systolic blood pressure greater than 140 mmHg, a diastolic blood pressure greater than 90 mmHg, or taking blood pressure medication.

Another 16% of all adults have high cholesterol (240 mg/dl or above), doubling their risk for heart disease,[18] and increasing the risk for stroke by 2 to 3 times.[19] Today, 1 in 8 older adults have Alzheimer's disease. If the current rate continues, there will be 6.7 million people with Alzheimer's by 2025.[20] When we break it down, 75% of health care costs are associated with chronic illness.[21] We can help ourselves and the nation by focusing on actions that reduce our health risks and lead to a healthier population.

Hope

Many of these illnesses can be prevented or their onset delayed with life changes. Actually, modern medical cures have played a relatively minor role in increasing adult lifespan. After examining the results of a longitudinal study, Friedman and Martin (2011) noted that people who have enjoyed good health care and a measure of wealth have only seen their life expectancy increase by 4 or 5 years over the past half century. The increase in life expectancy for most of the population appears to be the result of better housing, nutrition, safety (such as seat belts), and sanitation. The best surgical procedures and the most powerful pharmaceuticals of today are considered very successful if they extend life for several years. This is not to say that organ transplants and medical technology are not helpful to those who need them. But the key to better health for the majority of Americans lies in the decisions made about the pathways followed in life. These have a much greater impact in determining the length and quality of our lives.[22]

What determines your health?

The health you enjoy (or suffer from) is a product of your genetic composition, life experiences, and the decisions you make.

Nonmodifiable Risk Factors (Genetics and Experience)

Your genetic makeup and past experiences increase your risk for heart disease, cancer, stroke, and dementia, since we have no control over these they are called nonmodifiable risk factors. Examples of nonmodifiable risk factors are ones age, race, and gender. Our risk for disease increases as we age. The risk for stroke doubles each decade after the age of 55,[23] and the risk for Al-

> But who are you, O man, to answer back to God? Will what is molded say to its molder, "Why have you made me like this?"
>
> Romans 9:20

zheimer's Disease doubles every 5 years after reaching age 75.[24] Approximately 5-10% of people over age 65 have dementia, and anywhere from 22-65% have mild cognitive impairment, its primary precursor. Forty percent of all Americans over the age of 90 have dementia, which is the most common reason for nursing home placement.[25]

Your genetic makeup affects your health. Even if you are currently healthy, having a sibling who has a heart attack increases the likelihood you will experience a heart problem by 20% if you are male and 7% if you are female. The younger your sibling is when coronary heart

> "Bad genes" have only a modest impact on the lifespan of most people (20 to 30%). Most genetic influence is exerted in a person's older ages.

disease develops, the greater your risk for developing heart problems.[26] Further, having a first-degree relative (father, mother, brother, sister, child) who experiences a stroke before the age of 70 increases one's risk for stroke by about 75%.[27] Before we despair over "bad genes" consider that only a modest amount of the overall variation in lifespan (20 to 30%) is due to genetic factors.[28] Genetic influences on lifespan are minimal before the age of 60 and exert their effects primarily on older ages.[29]

Experiences and Exposures

Life experiences also play a role in our health. Exposure to toxins like lead paint or second hand smoke increase ones susceptibility to disease as well as stressful experiences like trauma or divorce. A study of middle-aged women indicated that of those who had experienced past physical, emotional, or sexual abuse, 34% of them were twice as likely as other women their age to have high blood pressure, high blood sugar, a large waist line, and poor cholesterol levels.[30] Similarly, a sample of adults who experienced physical or sexual abuse or neglect have been compared to a sample of adults who had not, and found them to be more likely to develop diabetes, lung disease, and vision problems.[31]

The types of toxins we are exposed to affect us as well. Environmental causes of cancer include tobacco, chemicals, radiation, and viruses. Sometimes 10 or more years may elapse between exposure to the toxin and a mutation that results in detectable cancer.[32]

Modifiable Risk Factors (Decisions)

We cannot change our age, genes, past experiences, or exposure to toxins but we do have control over what we decide to eat (and how much), whether we are active or not, and how we behave. These factors are modifiable risk factors that often exert more influence on our health. Consider, the decision to overeat, combined with eating bad foods while being physically inactive can lead to obesity (now the second leading cause of death in the US, following smoking).[33] Approximately one-third of cancer deaths are related to being overweight or obese, lack of physical activity, and poor nutrition.[34]

In a study, the risk of colorectal cancer was found to have increased in those who were obese, physically inactive, and who consumed a diet high in red or processed meat and low in fruits and vegetables. On the other hand, the risk was decreased in those who consumed a more nutritional diet. The risk of prostate cancer increases with obesity but decreases among those who eat a diet high in vegetables, especially tomato products (which contain lycopene).[35]

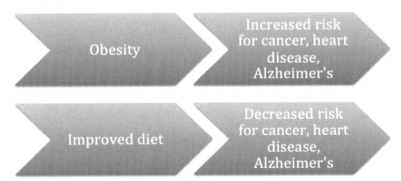

It is no surprise that modifiable risky behavior increases the risk of death by resulting in unintentional injuries. In fact, unintentional injuries rank fifth as an overall cause of death in the United States with 40.6 deaths per 1,000 (5% of all deaths—the largest culprit is automobile accidents).[36]

Other modifiable behaviors include smoking and drinking alcohol. Approximately 87% of lung cancer deaths are due to smoking, and smoking is the cause of about 30% of all cancer deaths.[37] Women who

> Who has woe? Who has sorrow? Who has strife? Who has complaining? Who has wounds without cause? Who has redness of eyes? Those who tarry long over wine; those who go to try mixed wine.
>
> *Proverbs 23:29-30*

consume one or more alcoholic drinks per day are at an increased risk of developing breast cancer.[38] Drinking alcohol is the actual cause for 3.5% of all deaths in the United States.[39]

> They make their tongue sharp as a serpent's, and under their lips is the venom of asps.
>
> *Psalm 140:3*

Even our relationships affect our health. When someone experiences negative emotions, a hormonal response is triggered in the body that can increase disease susceptibility by increasing cortisol and catecholamine. Increases in serum cortisol have been found to allow the reactivation of latent viruses.[40] Negative relationships are like a poisonous venom.

Given the role of the immune system in identifying and destroying abnormal cells, negative relationships have long been suspected of increasing the risk of developing cancer or promoting its spread.[41] In short, bad life decisions can place us on a path to poor health.

> *Or do you not know that your body is a temple of the Holy Spirit within you, whom you have from God? You are not your own, for you were bought with a price. So glorify God in your body.*
>
> *1 Corinthians 6:19-20*

Therapeutic Life Changes (TLCs)

On the other hand, Therapeutic Life Changes (TLCs) can improve your health, reverse the impact of bad decisions, and mitigate the impact of bad genes and experiences. You are never too old or in too poor health for TLCs to positively influence your health.

Consider Alzheimer's disease and Dementia, both have a strong genetic component. While 70% of the risk factor for these diseases is genetic, diabetes and obesity are the most significant non-genetic factors. However, it appears Alzheimer's may be prevented or delayed by engaging in TLCs like light or regular exercise such as walking or playing sports, and the performance of jobs that involve persuasion, mentoring, instruction, and supervision. Education also appears to push back onset of Alzheimer's.[42] Jennifer Manly of Columbia University Medical Center suggests, "With behavioral interventions to manage diet and exercise, we may see improvements in cognitive health and reduction in Alzheimer's prevalence."[43]

Do you find yourself at risk for heart disease or stroke? A reduction of blood pressure below 140-mmHg systolic and 90 mmHg diastolic would reduce your chances of having a stroke by 28 to as high as 44%, and your risk for coronary artery disease by 20-35%.[45]

> Being more physically active has been found to decrease stroke risk by 14 to as high as 40% depending on the intensity of the physical activity.[44]

A meta-analysis of clinical trials determined that for every 10% decrease in low-density lipoprotein (the bad cholesterol), there is a 10% reduction in heart attacks.[46]

TLCs

- ➤ Target disease with the greatest morbidity and mortality
- ➤ Very potent
- ➤ No side effects

Little changes go a long way toward placing us on the path to better health. TLCs tend to target the diseases with the greatest mortality and morbidity: cardiovascular disorders, cancer, obesity, and diabetes. TLCs put the individual in charge of their own health and there are no nasty side effects.[47]

Which TLCs work?

We can learn from longitudinal studies about TLCs that lead to better health. Long ago, a psychologist named Lewis Terman studied 1,500 bright boys and girls who were born around 1910. Most of the participants have passed away, and researchers have documented when and how they died. Their lives have been studied over the decades in great detail, and researchers have identified certain habits and patterns of living that propelled those who lived long lives. A smaller but somewhat similar study was the Harvard Study of Adult Development, which followed about 250 men over the decades after they attended Harvard in the 1930s. They too found habits and patterns that propelled those who lived the longest.[48]

The 10 TLCs described in this booklet may surprise you. They were derived from research. However, it is interesting to see they also are found throughout the Scripture. Taken together, these can be used to put us on a path to better health.

TLCs That Work
1. Really go to church
2. Have a daily quiet time
3. Develop real relationships
4. Practice forgiveness
5. Practice joy and contentment
6. Develop an attitude of gratitude and giving
7. Be diligent
8. Sleep well
9. Be physically active
10. Eat a proper diet

Therapeutic Life Changes

The first three TLCs actually address spiritual health. When people talk about health, they usually begin with a discussion of diet and exercise. However, spiritual health is a good foundation for physical health. In an examination of 42 studies that involved 126,000 participants, the results indicated that religious involvement increased survival by 29%.[49] Another meta-analysis (a study of studies) involving 21 studies and 107,910 participants, indicated that religious attendance was associated with a 37% increase in survival.[50] Though these studies involved many religious practices, a large number of the participants would characterize themselves as Christians and their religious attendance consisted of attending church services.

Today, fewer than 10% of those under the age of 30 regularly attend worship services.[51] Many are quick to point out that one need not be involved in organized religion or attend church services to be spiritually healthy. However, research indicates that involvement in religious activities (e.g., church attendance) is tied to better physical health.

> *And let us consider how to stir up one another to love and good works, not neglecting to meet together, as is the habit of some, but encouraging one another, and all the more as you see the Day drawing near.*
>
> *Hebrews 10:24-25*

1. Really go to Church

People who attend a religious service weekly and appear to be intrinsically motivated (attend based on a devotion to God rather than for an ulterior motive), receive a health benefit. Consider a nine-year national mortality study with a sample of 21,204 adults of all ages. Though there are many measures of good health, how long one lives seems to be the best, and therefore was the focus of these researchers. Those who did not attend religious services lived to an average age of 77. On the other hand, those attending religious services weekly or more lived to an average age of 82.[52]

African Americans tend to have poorer health and higher mortality rates than whites, but religious attendance appears to mitigate these factors and is associated with better health and greater life satisfaction for African Americans.[53] This study validated previous research showing the impact was even greater for the African Americans in the sample. Their life expectancy was 80 years of age for weekly attenders of religious services compared to 66 years of age for non-attenders, a fourteen-year difference![54]

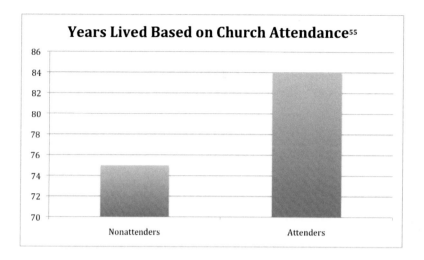

Years Lived Based on Church Attendance[55]

Another study examined the risk for death over a twenty-eight year period. This long study with 5,286 people of all ages indicated that the likelihood of dying for weekly attenders of religious services was 36% less during follow-up than non-attenders.[56] Clearly, there is a relationship between good health and religious attendance.

> A study of 3,968 adults ages 64-101 years in North Carolina after an average 6.3 year follow-up period indicated that the risk of dying was 46% less (49% less for women) for those who attended religious services.[57]

Why does this work?

> For the wrath of God is revealed from heaven against all ungodliness and unrighteousness of men, who by their unrighteousness suppress the truth.
>
> Romans 1:18

Why does attending church services have such a robust impact upon health? Some have hypothesized that the key is the social relationships built from attendance. Others have suggested that those who regularly attend church are less likely to smoke, drink alcohol, or engage in sexually promiscuous behaviors. Certainly, these are aspects to the health benefit. However, it also appears that church attendance increases positive health behaviors like giving and gratitude.[58]

There also appears to be a boost from participation in the actual church service. In studies of health and religiousness, 80% of them have indicated links between religiousness and measures of well-being such as life satisfaction, happiness, positive affect, or high morale. Participation in services fosters hope, optimism, and joy by increasing social support, and by giving life meaning and purpose.[59]

So, instead of lacing up tennis shoes and heading to the gym on a Sunday morning it appears one would be wise to pick up the Bible and head to church if their goal is better health. I once asked Dr. Harold Koenig, a Duke University research psychiatrist, and the leader in research in this area if he thought simply going to church would lead to better health. You can view his response online at www.EdwardMoody.com. In essence, he said, yes if one ends up going for intrinsic reasons. How can your church attendance help your physical health?

a. Focus on God

You must be truly focused upon God. Gordon Allport studied religious devotion back in the 1950s. He described two types of religious

| Edward Moody interview
with Harold Koenig
www.EdwardMoody.com |

people. There are those with an extrinsic orientation that use religion to obtain some non-spiritual goal like finding friends or achieving social status, prestige, and power (or even improving one's health). Then there are those with an intrinsic orientation

| But seek first the kingdom of God and his righteousness, and all these things will be added to you.
Matthew 6:33 |

who are religious for the sake of religion. Their strong faith is the principal motivating force in their everyday lives. Their faith affects their behavior, decisions, and is characterized by a close relationship with God.

It is individuals with intrinsic faith that generally have lower incidents of cancer, chronic anxiety, and measurable depression. In fact, intrinsic religiosity is a stronger factor than social status or financial security in determining elderly people's self-perceived well-being and life satisfaction.[60] So help your health by attending church and begin by focusing completely on God.[61]

b. Focus on the Service

Enjoy and fully participate in the service. Focus upon the positive aspects of the church you attend and the activities that are performed. Rather than focusing upon something you may dislike such as worship style, consider how you are part of a worship tradition with a 2,000-year heritage. Think about the Scripture being read, the lyrics that are sung as well as the message delivered. Read along in the text and take notes during the message. In addition to the spiritual benefit, an individual is stimulated cognitively which leads to measurable results. Several studies suggest that religious involvement may forestall the development of cognitive impairment in older adults and may even influence the progression of Alzheimer's disease.[62]

A cognitive psychologist (Yonker, 2010) has speculated upon this phenomenon and concluded that participation in services helps an individual because it preserves the five major types of memory: procedural, semantic, episodic, priming, and working.

Procedural memory involves skills and habits that stay with a person and are recalled with little effort after they are learned. Participation in a church service stimulates procedural memory by the singing of familiar hymns

And all the people gathered as one man . . . And they told Ezra the scribe to bring the Book of the Law of Moses . . . So Ezra the priest brought the Law before the assembly . . . And he read from it . . . in the presence of the men and the women and those who could understand. And the ears of all the people were attentive to the Book of the Law. And Ezra the scribe stood on a wooden platform that they had made for the purpose. . . . And Ezra blessed the LORD, the great God, and all the people answered, "Amen, Amen," lifting up their hands. And they bowed their heads and worshiped the LORD with their faces to the ground. Also Jeshua, Bani, . . . helped the people to understand the Law . . . They read from the book, from the Law of God, clearly, and they gave the sense, so that the people understood the reading.

Nehemiah 8:1-8

from memory, repeating standard liturgical responses during a service, or praying memorized prayers.

Semantic memory involves general knowledge one accrues during their lifetime. Semantic memory is aided by thinking about Bible stories and Bible characters. This is often utilized in Sunday School or Bible study classes as well as during the message at a church service.

Episodic memory is personally relevant memory and is used when recalling how past or present situations might be relevant to a particular Scripture or sermon topic. This is aided when one considers how to apply a passage to a particular issue in life.

Priming memory is where a stimulus activates a memory that does not require conscious retrieval, such as the cross that activates thoughts about Jesus' sacrifice or the elements of the Eucharist where one ponders the meaning of the bread or the cup.

Working memory is used when thinking about incoming information. This is stimulated when considering and following the logical points of a pastor's sermon or contemplating complex religious concepts such as the Trinity or Heaven. This involvement by stimulating these different areas of memory may help to slow cognitive decline that comes with age or diseases like Alzheimer's disease or Dementia.[63]

So also faith by itself, if it does not have works, is dead.

James 2:17

---

c. Focus on Serving

Become an usher, greeter, parking lot attendant, Scripture reader, Sunday School teacher, small group leader, volunteer janitor, nursery worker, or anything that requires you to get involved in your church. Church involvement appears to delay onset of disability.[64] There is something about having an important task to do and somewhere to be that keeps the mind and body working.

d. Focus on Other People

Develop relationships at your place of worship so there are people you look forward to seeing. Follow the lives of others. When you go to church, you want to have anticipation like, "I wonder

> *Religion that is pure and undefiled before God, the Father, is this: to visit orphans and widows in their afflicton, and to keep oneself unstained from the world.*
>
> *James 1:27*

if Jim and Jane have had their baby yet," and "will Linda keep dating that fellow George?" Reach outside of yourself. Visit people when they are in the hospital. Get to know other people by going out to dinner with them. Make the effort to discuss spiritual topics with them. Take someone "under your wing" and mentor him or her, performing the function Paul described in Titus 2.

This type of involvement leads to a larger network of friends and results in better coping skills. This is probably why many studies report that religious activities are related to better coping and greater quality of life among patients with cancer.[65] The positive emotional states resulting from these beneficial personal relationships is part of the boost received from involvement in church.[66]

e. Focus on Yourself

As you worship look at yourself, especially during communion. Pausing to take part in communion allows us to take stock of our lives and address issues like bitterness, anger, and unforgiveness in our hearts as well as behaviors (e.g., drinking, gluttony, sexual immorality) that can negatively impact our health. It is good to take the time for communion on a regular basis.

> *For as often as you eat this bread and drink the cup, you proclaim the Lord's death until he comes. Whoever, therefore, eats the bread or drinks the cup of the Lord in an unworthy manner will be guilty concerning the body and blood of the Lord. Let a person examine himself, then, and so eat of the bread and drink of the cup. For anyone who eats and drinks without discerning the body eats and drinks judgment on himself. That is why many of you are weak and ill, and some have died. But if we judged ourselves truly, we would not be judged. But when we are judged by the Lord, we are disciplined so that we may not be condemned along with the world.*
>
> *1 Corinthians 11:26-32*

> "I think I can safely say that the Judeo-Christian Bible is a self-help book that probably enabled more people to make more extensive and intensive personality and behavior changes than all professional therapists combined."
>
> **Albert Ellis**[67]

2. Have a Daily Quiet Time of Scripture Reading and Prayer

A second TLC is to pause for Bible reading and prayer. Famed psychologist Albert Ellis, who was no friend of Christianity, observed that the Bible was very helpful when it came to helping others. The

> "For years I have read my Bible through once a year. I read it every morning, as the very best way to begin the day."
>
> John Quincy Adams

research supports his assertion. In one study, private religious activity (meditation, prayer, or Bible study) was examined over a six-year period and found to be helpful. Those who did not participate in these activities were

> This Book of the Law shall not depart from your mouth, but you shall meditate on it day and night, so that you may be careful to do according to all that is written in it. For then you will make your way prosperous, and then you will have good success.
>
> Joshua 1:8

47% more likely to have died during follow-up.[68] How is that for encouragement to read your Bible and pray?

> And we know that for those who love God all things work together for good, for those who are called according to his purpose.
>
> Romans 8:28

A. Read Your Bible Every Day

Other research has examined the relationship between private religious activities (prayer, religious coping, or Bible study) and found a positive impact upon blood pressure.[69] Why do these kinds of activities have such a potent health impact? Perhaps Scripture reading and prayer have a calming effect that is the source of these findings. People who have a greater purpose and meaning or a

> **Sense of Coherance**
>
> The sense that the world is predictable and comprehensible, that one has the ability to meet the demands of one's environment, and that challenges have meaning and purpose.[71]

sense of coherence have better health. For example, having greater purpose and meaning in life may protect against both Alzheimer's disease and mild cognitive impairment in older persons.[70] Further, a sense of coherence may mitigate the impact of anxiety, stress, negative thinking, and a tendency to catastrophize.[72]

> *For the word of God is living and active, sharper than any two-edged sword, piercing to the division of soul and of spirit, of joints and of marrow, and discerning the thoughts and intentions of the heart.*
>
> *Hebrews 4:12*

a. Get a Handle on Anxiety

Anxiety can be deadly. Approximately one-third of US adults report experiencing high levels of stress.[73] In one study chronic anxiety predicted a 43% increase in the chance of having a heart attack[74], and more than doubles the risk of death from lung cancer.[75]

> NK or Natural Killer cells strengthen the immune system in the body. When they are weakened one is at greater risk for cancer and other health problems.

Psychological stress and negative emotions have been associated with a number of adverse metabolic states including insulin resistance, and impaired natural killer (NK) cell activity.[76] Prolonged stress is linked to poor health and premature death. What we think about stress is very important. In a large study (28,753 participants), 55% of the participants indicated experiencing moderate to high levels of stress within the past year, and 33.7% of them said the stress had negatively impacted their health. Those who reported higher stress and beliefs that the stress negatively impacted their health had a 43% increased risk of premature death.[77] The health damage to us as a result of stress seems to be tied to worry.

Reading the Bible can help alleviate this. As an example, consider Matthew 6.

> *Therefore I tell you, do not be anxious about your life, what you will eat or what you will drink, nor about your body, what you will put on. Is not life more than food, and the body more than clothing?*
>
> *Matthew 6:25*

The passage admonishes us not to be anxious and instructs us on what life is all about.

> *And which of you by being anxious can add a single hour to his span of life?*
>
> *Matthew 6:27*

The futility of anxiety and worry is described.

> *Look at the birds of the air: they neither sow nor reap nor gather into barns, and yet your heavenly Father feeds them. Are you not of more value than they?*
>
> *Matthew 6:26*

The reader receives an object lesson about dealing with anxiety. When you see a bird or flower, you can be reminded of God's care for you.

> *But seek first the kingdom of God and his righteousness, and all these things will be added to you.*
>
> *Matthew 6:33*

The reader is instructed that if they will focus on God, the rest will fall into place.

> *Therefore do not be anxious about tomorrow, for tomorrow will be anxious for itself. Sufficient for the day is its own trouble.*
>
> *Matthew 6:34*

Rather than worrying, deal with the issue at hand. Following these instructions can stop anxiety or negative thinking before it grows into catastrophizing. In the Terman study, the catastrophizers generally could not face their problems. They were clearly more likely to die from accidents or violence, and on an especially dangerous path.[78] The reading and application of Scripture can go far in combatting these feelings.

Similar to ones motivation to attend church, it appears the intrinsic desire to know God leads to a sense of coherence, which buffers the difficulties one experiences upon the road of life. This lessens the likelihood one will suffer from debilitating anxiety and catastrophic or negative thinking. Scripture helps us make sense of the world.

> *And do not fear those who kill the body but cannot kill the soul. Rather fear him who can destroy both soul and body in hell.*
>
> *Matthew 10:28*

b. Read and Obtain a Proper Perspective on Health

Reading the Scripture can help one have a realistic perspective on life and health. Examples in the Scripture like that of Hezekiah (2 Kings 20) can help us put our health into perspective. After being told to "put his house in order," he prayed and received an extension of his life. He faltered during that time at great cost to his descendants. Sometimes good health can dull us into a sense of complacency. A healthy Hezekiah was not necessarily a better Hezekiah.

> *Not only that, but we rejoice in our sufferings, knowing that suffering produces endurance, and endurance produces character, and character produces hope, and hope does not put us to shame, because God's love has been poured into our hearts through the Holy Spirit who has been given to us.*
>
> *Romans 5:3-5*

We are likely to have health problems at some point in life. Paul's writings help us when we are ill; reminding us that God is producing endurance, character, and hope in us. When you are ill, if you are a believer, you can meditate upon how God is with you and helps you.

c. Read the Passion

Suppose you feel alone and as if no one cares about you, you can read the gospels and see how Jesus was not indifferent. He appears especially concerned for those who suffer (Matthew 8:6-7, 16-17; Matthew 9:20-22, 35; Matthew 15:30; Matthew 19:1-2, and 1 Peter 2:24). Sometimes we feel as if no one really understands our plight. The Scripture teaches us that God gets it. Passages on the suffering of Christ help us see this.

Jesus Gets It

He was despised and rejected by men; a man of sorrows, and acquainted with grief; and as one from whom men hide their faces he was despised, and we esteemed him not.

Isaiah 53:3

Surely he has borne our griefs and carried our sorrows; yet we esteemed him stricken, smitten by God, and afflicted. But he was pierced for our transgressions; he was crushed for our iniquities; upon him was the chastisement that brought us peace, and with his wounds we are healed.

Isaiah 53:4-5

And being in an agony he prayed more earnestly; and his sweat became like great drops of blood falling down to the ground.

Luke 22:44

Scriptures also teach us to expect suffering, and that we have something better than this life to look forward to.

Beloved, do not be surprised at the fiery trial when it comes upon you to test you, as though something strange were happening to you. But rejoice insofar as you share Christ's sufferings, that you may also rejoice and be glad when his glory is revealed.

1 Peter 4:12-13

It is important to see the whole of all of Scripture rather than only looking at parts. Some have taken Bible passages out of context and refused medical treatment in an effort to demonstrate their faith.[79] Perhaps it is helpful to look at passages like Paul's to

Timothy where he instructed Timothy to take wine (the medicine of his day) for the sake of his stomach to help us follow through with medical treatment.

> *No longer drink only water, but use a little wine for the sake of your stomach and your frequent ailments.*
>
> *1 Timothy 5:23*

Religious people who are struggling with their faith are also at greater risk. A study of hospitalized patients examined the characteristics of survivors and compared them to patients that died. Those that experienced religious struggle (feeling abandoned or punished by God, questioning God's love and power, feeling abandoned by church, feeling the devil caused their health problem) had an increased risk of death (6% higher for every 1-point increase on 21-point religious struggle scale).[80]

> *My God, my God, why have you forsaken me? Why are you so far from saving me, from the words of my groaning?*
>
> *Psalm 22:1*

Scripture helps us with these kinds of concerns. There are passages in the Psalms that address just this kind of problem, and we could pray these Psalms as prayers of our own. Further, counsel from a trusted pastor can address these kinds of issues as well as studying the lives of biblical characters like Job.

> *As an example of suffering and patience, brothers, take the prophets who spoke in the name of the Lord. Behold, we consider those blessed who remained steadfast. You have heard of the steadfastness of Job, and you have seen the purpose of the Lord, how the Lord is compassionate and merciful.*
>
> *James 5:10-11*

A reader of the Bible will see that good people do suffer, and we can use the manner in which they handled their suffering as a model in our own life.

B. Pray Throughout the Day

Reading Scripture goes hand in hand with prayer. Take a few minutes throughout the day to pray. Praying helps produce the sense of coherence that leads to better health. We are likely to benefit from better blood pressure and perhaps a stronger NK cell response when we pray. If prayer is new to you, use the Model Prayer as a guide.

> . . . When you pray, go into your room and shut the door and pray to your Father who is in secret. And your Father who sees in secret will reward you.
>
> Matthew 6:6

Find your own personal and private place to pray. This can be your kitchen table, your car, or a spot in the outdoors. Your prayers are between you and God. They are personal, private, and valuable.

> . . . when you pray, do not heap up empty phrases.
>
> Matthew 6:7

Your prayers need not be long, but they do need to be sincere.

> Pray then like this:
> Our Father in heaven, hallowed be your name.
>
> Matthew 6:9

Start by honoring and praising God. You might praise God for His attributes (which you learn about from reading Scripture). You might thank Him for what He has done.

> Your kingdom come, your will be done, on earth as it is in heaven.
>
> Matthew 6:10

Then pray for God's will (Your will be done). Look for guidance in any decision you might be facing. Use prayer to make needed changes in your life. Pray that God will give you the proper perspective.

> *Give us this day our daily bread.*
>
> *Matthew 6:11*

Pray about your needs (Give us this day) and anything that concerns you. Pray for forgiveness (forgive us our debts). Ask God to search your heart and show you what needs to be rooted out.

> *And forgive us our debts, as we also have forgiven our debtors.*
>
> *Matthew 6:12*

Pray for others. Pray for each of these you have: parents, spouse, children, grandchildren, and friends. At times, pray for coworkers, those with whom you worship, neighbors, and extended family. It appears that people who regularly pray and trust God acquire an indirect sense of control when they are ill. In a study of hospitalized patients, those who rated highest on religious coping showed the lowest level of depression indicating they were coping well with the stress of their illness. Even the severely ill experienced this benefit.[81]

> *. . . 'You shall love your neighbor as yourself,' There is no other commandments greater than these.*
>
> *Mark 12:31*

3. Develop Real Relationships

Real relationships lead to a healthier path. Real relationships may consist of close friends, a cohesive marriage, strong family ties, or a combination of these. For some time having relationships has been seen as important to physical health. In a classic study examining social support, Berkman and Syme (1979) found that having good relationships with strong social contacts led to a longer life (on average of 2.8 years longer for women and 2.3 years longer for men) than those who had few social contacts.[82]

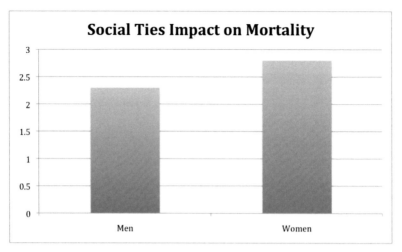

Social Ties Impact on Mortality

Loneliness

Being isolated appears to be especially dangerous. Even in healthy medical students, feelings of loneliness has been linked to lower NK cell activity, higher urinary cortisol, and

> *Whoever isolates himself seeks his own desire; he breaks out against all sound judgment.*
>
> *Proverbs 18:1*

conditions which lead to a weakened immune system increasing ones vulnerability to health problems.[83]

When one looks closer at the health of those who tend to be socially isolated, they find them to have a higher risk for blood pressure problems[84], and to be more susceptible to inflammatory markers, which are precursors to various diseases.[85]

Social isolation has been related to cardiovascular disease where there is a higher mortality rate for socially isolated individuals. In fact, the risk of cardiac death is almost two and one-half times greater for those with 3 or fewer people in their social support network, compared to those with larger networks.[86]

In a study of patients for 29 months after a heart attack, those who reported low social support had an 80% increased risk of death or recurrent heart attack, and an increased all-cause mortality risk by 150%.[87]

Loneliness Decreased NK Cell Activity

Lacking real relationships has been linked to an increased risk for cancer. A study of John Hopkins University medical students over a sixteen year period indicated that those identified as loners who suppressed their emotions were 16 times more likely to develop cancer later in life.[88] Lacking close relationships has been linked to cognitive decline. This may be the result of the presence of the hormone cortisol, which has been implicated as a cause of cognitive problems.[89]

On the other hand, extensive research has been conducted on breast cancer and social support. In over 70% of the studies there has been a significant positive association between social support and survival.[90] The temptation is to do anything one can to find anyone who might be a companion or friend. But it is important to note that the health benefit only emerges with the right type of relationship.

> Whoever walks with the wise becomes wise, but the companion of fools will suffer harm.
>
> Proverbs 13:20

In Friedman and Martin's examination of the Terman subjects, they found that those who were sociable did not live longer than those who were not. They noted that the sociable subjects were more likely to drink and smoke and frequent environments where drinking and smoking were a way of life. On the other hand, another type of sociable person tended to connect emotionally with others in a powerful way. These were the ones who were likely to experience good health.[91] The key appears to be relationships of substance rather than superficiality.

The Harvard Study of Adult Development indicated it was the men who maintained deep social relationships and stable marriages that had the best health.[92] In fact, happily married husbands and wives are up to three times more likely than their unmarried counterparts to be alive 15 years after heart bypass surgery.[93] Further, morbidity and mortality from cancer is lower among married compared to unmarried people.[94]

> He who finds a wife finds a good thing and obtains favor from the Lord.
>
> Proverbs 18:22
>
> An excellent wife is the crown of her husband, but she who brings shame is like rottenness in his bones.
>
> Proverbs 12:4

> *Two are better than one, because they have a good reward for their toil. For if they fall, one will lift up his fellow. But woe to him who is alone when he falls and has not another to lift him up! Again, if two lie together, they keep warm, but how can one keep warm alone? And though a man might prevail against one who is alone, two will withstand him—a threefold cord is not quickly broken.*
>
> Ecclesiastes 4:9-11

How does this work?

Real relationships help buffer against the stress and difficulties of life. Interestingly, this can even be seen in children. In one study, schoolchildren in fifth and sixth grade were given journals to record their feelings throughout the day, and their saliva was tested four times a day. Results indicated that having a best friend present during a stressful experience significantly buffered the children against the negative effects of experiences. The cortisol levels (as measured in the saliva) and self-worth (as noted in the journals) remained unchanged in the children who reported having a best friend. However, when a best friend was not present, there was an increase in cortisol and a decrease in self-worth.[95]

Having a friend provide social support assists with the coping process and counteracts the negative effects on blood pressure as well.[96] A study of adults with mild hypertension, indicated that those with strong cohesive marriages had significantly lower diastolic blood pressure than those with low marital support.[97]

Similarly, in a study of individuals who experienced chronic job strain, the results indicated that those who had friends that helped them cope had lower blood pressure during follow-up. On the other hand, those who had few friends and little social support had a significant increase in blood pressure.[98]

The impact of real relationships is stronger than well-established risk factors for chronic diseases and mortality, such as smoking, blood pressure, lipids, obesity, and physical inactivity. In some cases, real relationships may help stave off illness altogether.[99]

A man of many companions may come to ruin, but there is a friend who sticks closer than a brother.

Proverbs 18:24

What does one do?

Develop Companion Friendships

How do you know if you have a real relationship that will lead to better health? One key is that you will have someone with whom you can confide. Not having a friend one can confide in has been found to increase risk for heart attack by 34%.[101] On the other hand, having a close confidant is associated with greater psychological well-being.

Therefore, confess your sins to one another and pray for one another, that you may be healed. The prayer of a righteous person has great power as it is working.

James 5:16

Companion friends are characterized by a high degree of self-disclosure (telling each other what they would not share with others), and a high degree of openness, honesty, truthfulness, and trust. Companion friends share things they value highly, like their plans, hopes, dreams, ambitions, and interests.

Iron sharpens iron, and one man sharpens another.

Proverbs 27:17

Companion friends often try to emulate what they admire in their counterpart. They actively encourage and spur one another on to greater self-awareness and personal growth by investing time and effort in each other.

> *Therefore encourage one another and build*
> *one another up, just as you are doing.*
>
> *1 Thessalonians 5:11*

People who go to church regularly are more likely to have this kind of friend. Indeed this is why many researchers believe regular church attenders live longer than those who do not.

Friend → **Feeling part of the church** → **Grateful to God** → **Better health** → **Friend**

People who are part of a church where they have this kind of friend are more likely to feel a part of the congregation (84% indicated this in one sample). They are also more likely to feel grateful to God and have better health.[102] This type of friend does not develop quickly. It is developed slowly over a period of frequent contact, such as worship services and surrounding activities.

Nothing Can Replace a Real Relationship

Interestingly, though many believe money would make them happy, the research indicates it can't replace real relationships. Research conducted on people with a net worth of $25 million or more indicates that their number one concern was a sense of isolation. The greater the wealth, the greater the sense of isolation. The main lacking in their lives were the friendships and support that helps to get one through difficult times.[103]

Some have suggested that pets can meet the needs of a relationship. Indeed, companion animals can enrich our lives. Animal interactions have been shown to reduce blood pressure, lower

> *Whoever is righteous has regard for the life of his beast, but the mercy of the wicked is cruel.*
>
> Proverbs 12:10

cholesterol improve recovery from cardiovascular disease, help one exercise more, forestall symptoms of Alzheimer's disease, and prevent acute health crises, such as seizures and panic attacks.[104] However, the Terman results indicated that it is real relationships with people rather than pets that really impacted the longevity of their subjects. Those who had pets were not more likely to survive than those who did not.[105] Though a pet can be helpful, they are no substitute for a real relationship with another person.

> *Then the Lord God said, "It is not good that the man should be alone; I will make him a helper fit for him."*
>
> Genesis 2:18

4. Practice Forgiveness

> *For if you <u>forgive others</u> their trespasses, your heavenly Father will also forgive you, but if you do not <u>forgive others</u> their trespasses, neither will your Father forgive your trespasses.*
>
> Matthew 6:14-15

A key TLC is to practice forgiveness. Refusing to forgive others is dangerous. When we do not wish to forgive another person, we often say things like, "They don't deserve to be forgiven" or "They haven't asked to be forgiven" as if forgiveness is about the other person. This is what researchers refer to as "conditional forgiveness." In Scripture, Jesus commanded, "Forgive others their trespasses" making no reference to what the others may or may not have done.

An interesting research study published in the *Journal of Behavioral Medicine* indicated that conditional forgiveness is a significant predictor of death because of the impact failing to forgive has upon a person's health. The researchers entitled their study "Forgive to live." People who placed a condition on whether they would forgive may have shortened their lives.[106] Similar research has indicated that unforgiveness is associated with emotions, thoughts, and behaviors that have a negative impact on health.[107] Unforgiveness is fueled by anger and hostility. Hostility is strongly linked to cardiovascular disease and cardiovascular mortality. In one study, men with higher levels of anger (upper 20%) experienced 2.5 times more fatal heart attacks, fatal coronary artery disease, and angina than those in the lowest 20% after seven years later.[108]

What happens to a person physically when they harbor unforgiveness and hostility in their hearts? There is a negative impact on immune functioning, especially in women,[109] and an increase in the

> But if you bite and devour one another, watch out that you are not consummed by one another.
>
> Galatians 5:15

risk of developing hypertension which is a strong predictor of stroke.[110]

On the other hand, forgiveness appears to reduce heart problems,[111] and boost immune response. If you want to get on a path that leads to good health, you must learn to forgive others. But how?

> But I say to you, Do not resist the one who is evil. But if anyone slaps you on the right cheek, turn to him the other also.
>
> Matthew 5:39

a. Don't Keep Score

We are natural scorekeepers. Attend a ballgame between young children where the score is not being kept, and somewhere there will be several people keeping score. We are the same when it comes to interpersonal slights. It is tempting to keep track of those who have mistreated us or hurt us in some way. But, those who tend to blame others for their misfortunes and continue to harbor feelings of hostility experience impaired immunological and cardiovascular functioning.[112] Left unchecked, some are at risk for developing an unforgiving personality. In the Terman subjects, those who tended to react with hostility to interpersonal slights were particularly likely to suffer lingering physiological damage.[113]

> It is an honor for a man to keep aloof from strife, but every fool will be quarreling.
>
> Proverbs 20:3

It has been suggested that there is a forgiving personality that consists of agreeableness, emotional stability, and religiousness and spirituality. Highly agreeable people tend to thrive interpersonally and experience less conflict in relationships than less agreeable people do. The result is less negative emotion, and the tendency not to be moody or overly sensitive.[114]

With the Terman subjects, it was those who were less critical of others, tried to avoid arguments, and didn't always try to get things their way that tended to be healthier and live longer.[115]

b. Look for the Good

There are certain techniques that can help us forgive. In one study, researchers asked participants to think about a situation where they had been wronged. They were then asked to write about a possible benefit as a result of that situation.[116]

Processing the transgression and considering how one had benefited helped the participants to forgive. This sounds like the process Joseph engaged in as he dealt with his brother's offense against him. Though he was hurt by his brother's actions, he came to see how God used it for good.

> As for you, you meant evil against me, but God meant it for good, to bring it about that many people should be kept alive, as they are today.
>
> Genesis 50:20

Other research has indicated that people who are able to have empathy for the offender are better able to forgive. For example, one might think that an offender did not truly understand the impact of their behavior or lacked the knowledge and training of others. This reminds me of Jesus' words in His statement about those who crucified Him.

> And Jesus said, "Father, forgive them, for they know not what they do."
>
> Luke 23:34a

When people forgive, they tend to attribute the transgressor as more likable and give them "the benefit of the doubt."[117]

c. Move On

It is hard to forgive when one ruminates about the offense against them. Rumination involves the tendency to experience intrusive thoughts, affect, and images about past events, which hinder forgiveness.[118] Though it is hard to forgive,

> Take every thought captive to obey Christ.
>
> 2 Corinthians 10:5b

it is important to remember the LORD has indicated to us that it is possible. We must forgive and move on.

> But Jesus looked at them and said, "With man this is impossible, but with God all things are possible."
>
> Matthew 19:26

d. Think About How You Have Been Forgiven

It seems to be easier to forgive others when we consider our own transgressions. Think about times when people have forgiven you for various transgressions. Also, focus upon how God has forgiven you.

> Bearing with one another and, if one has a complaint against another, forgiving each other; as the Lord has forgiven you, so you also must forgive.
>
> Colossians 3:13

Forgiveness is not

It is important to think about what forgiveness is not. Forgiveness is not forgetting. It is impossible to forget what someone has done to us. The Scriptures (especially Proverbs) teach us to learn from our interactions from others and to avoid certain people based on this. Forgiveness is not excusing bad behavior. The Scripture teaches us to hold others accountable for their actions and provides us instructions (Matthew 18) for how to do this. Finally, forgiveness is not reconciliation. Reconciliation requires cooperation from both parties. We cannot control what others may or may not do. Forgiveness is choosing not to hold a grudge or harbor ill will against someone who has wronged us.

> Rejoice in the Lord always; again I will say, rejoice.
>
> Philippians 4:4

5. Practice Joy and Contentment

Joy and contentment are tied to good health. The word joy is used nearly 200 times in Scripture and Paul instructed us that godliness with contentment is great gain. The closest measure to joy is opti-

> *A joyful heart is good medicine, but a crushed spirit dries up the bones.*
> Proverbs 17:22

mism and the closest measure to contentment is life satisfaction. Optimism (the generalized expectation that good things rather than bad things will happen) is related to measures of healthy cellular immunity when stressors are present suggesting that optimism can assuage the negative effects of stress on the immune system.[119]

Positive affect has been linked to physical health in numerous studies showing an increase in longevity. Positive affect is defined as joviality, self-assurance, and attentiveness. Positive af-

> Joyful, engaged individuals are better able to thrive and build positive bonds with others, especially compared to people who are dejected or depressed.[121]

fectivity may change how people perceive their health and bodies. Those higher with positive affectivity report fewer and less severe symptoms than those without it. It also leads to better sleep habits, increased exercise, and better coping skills.[120]

Positive affectivity sounds a lot like joy and contentment. It is found in those who are ill as well as those who feel well. People who are cheerful and optimistic are generally healthier. Women who scored in the top quartile of optimism (versus lowest quartile) had a 16% decrease in heart attack, a 14% decrease in all-cause mortality, and a 30% decrease in coronary heart disease mortality. Women who scored in the top quartile of cynical hostility (versus lowest quartile) had a 13% increase in risk of heart attack, and a 16% increase in all-cause mortality.[122]

Greater life satisfaction (the closest measure to contentment) is associated with a significantly lower likelihood of high blood pressure,[123] as is a cheerful, contented and satisfied, and happy disposition.[124] We can experience joy and contentment regardless of our circumstances. Our tendency is to think, "I would be happy if . . .," although the "if" never pleases. Instead we need to practice an attitude of "I will be joyful in spite of . . . ." Paul wrote to rejoice always.

> *Not that I am speaking of being in need, for I have learned in whatever situation I am to be content. I know how to be brought low, and I know how to abound. In any and every circumstance, I have learned the secret of facing plenty and hunger, abundance and need.*
>
> *Philippians 4:11-12*

a. Practice Joy in the Good Times and Bad

If we concentrate on what we have in God, we can have joy in the good and bad times. Joy must be practiced. The first step to practicing joy is to get a handle on your moods.

> *Whoever is slow to anger is better than the mighty, and he who rules his spirit than he who takes a city.*
>
> *Proverbs 16:32*

Shifting moods are natural. Daily fluctuations in mood have been found to affect ambulatory blood pressure measurements in those with normal blood pressure or mild hypertension.[125] However, it is important to rein these moods in. This is where Paul's admonishment to "think on these things" comes into play. Thoughts influence mood, which influences blood pressure for good or bad.

> *Finally, brothers, whatever is true, whatever is honorable, whatever is just, whatever is pure, whatever is lovely, whatever is commendable, if there is any excellence, if there is anything worthy of praise, think about these things.*
>
> *Philippians 4:8*

Paul instructs us to think on certain things. This is especially helpful in the age of instant news and Twitter, where our moods can be changed in a moment. If you find your joy being robbed, it may be necessary to take an email, Twitter, or news vacation.

b. Fast From an Email, Twitter, and/or Facebook

A study on people who agreed to ignore email for five days indicated that they were more productive and experienced less stress than those who did not take the "email vacation." Further, coworkers who continued reading emails had constant elevated heart rates, while the "vacationers" had more natural, variable heart rates.[126] You may not be able to do a complete email vacation. But choose certain times to fast from technology. When you find yourself being influenced from the information around you, get into the outdoors or go for a walk, which can elevate your mood. We can experience joy even in difficult circumstances.

> *A tranquil heart gives life to the flesh, but envy makes the bones rot.*
>
> *Proverbs 14:30*

c. Practice Contentment

The enemy of joy and contentment is envy. This is seen when we compare ourselves to others or covet what others have. This inflicts a terrible toil upon our body.

> *I perceived that there is nothing better for them than to be joyful and to do good as long as they live.*
>
> *Ecclesiastes 3:12*
>
> *But godliness with contentment is great again.*
>
> *1 Timothy 6:6*

To fight envy it is important to practice contentment. Concentrate upon what you have rather than comparing yourself with others. Interestingly, research has indicated the more we have the less happy we appear to be. This is likely because we tend to have higher expectations as the number of choices rises.[127] A further cause is that God made us for something more than things.

> "I would maintain that thanks are the highest form of thought, and that gratitude is happiness doubled by wonder."
>
> G. K. Chesterson[128]

6. Develop an Attitude of Gratitude and Giving

Many researchers have concluded that gratitude is one of the key components of the "good life." Gratitude is strongly associated with enhanced emotional well-being.[129] Appreciation has been found to have a significant influence upon some antibodies that defend the body from pathogens.[130] Those who report practicing gratitude report higher levels of alertness, vitality, and energy; spend more time exercising; report more hours of nightly sleep, and better quality sleep; report fewer headaches, coughing, nausea, and pain, and show a heightened immunity in both healthy and sick people.[131]

a. Count Your Blessings

Intentionally practice gratitude. In a six week intervention participants were randomly assigned to 1 of 3 experimental conditions (hassles, gratitude listing, and either neutral life events or social comparison). They recorded their mood, coping behaviors, health behaviors, physical symptoms, and overall life appraisals.[132]

Those in the gratitude group counted the blessings they received. Examples of blessings included "getting through my first set of midterms," "having supportive friends," "the car my dad bought me," "my parents telling me they love me." This worked. The gratitude groups exhibited better well-being than the comparison groups. The effect on positive affect appeared to be the most robust finding.[133] Grateful thinking promotes the savoring of positive life experiences and situations, so that the maximum satisfaction and enjoyment is extracted from the person's circumstances.[134]

I have been blessed by . . .
1.
2.
3.

I am thankful for . . .
1.
2.
3.

Job is an example of this. He told his wife in essence that they should praise God in the good times as well as the bad. Job did not appear to be a happy man, yet he likely experienced joy and gratitude as he suffered. Note his hope in the resurrection.

For I know that my Redeemer lives, and at the last he will stand upon the earth. And after my skin has been thus destroyed, yet in my flesh I shall see God.

Job 19:25-26

b. Go Beyond Thank You

When someone does something for you instead of just saying, "Thank you" reflect

Every week take the time to tell someone how important they are in your life.

upon what you have received and consider what it means to you. Then recognize the source of the action. Take the time to send a thank you note or explain to people how special they are to you. Let a coworker know how you appreciate them. Pray prayers of gratitude to God for the people in your life.

In all things I have shown you that by working hard in this way we must help the weak and remember the words of the Lord Jesus, how he himself said, "It is more blessed to give than to receive."

Acts 20:35

c. Focus on Giving Rather Than Getting

➤ 70% percent of all volunteering is done in a religious setting.

➤ Those who attend religious services are most likely to volunteer.

➤ Regular church attendees account for 80% of all charitable giving.[136]

I think many people laugh when they hear the words of Christ ("It is more blessed to give than to receive"), but the path to good health rolls through giving and serving. Performing acts of generosity appears to set the stage for good health. Generosity or altruism refers to a specific form of motivation for benefiting another. Volunteers experience significantly greater life satisfaction, a stronger will to live, and fewer symptoms of depression, anxiety, and physical illness compared to those who do not volunteer. Giving help to others is a substantially stronger predictor of good mental health than receiving help.[137]

Volunteering and other altruistic activities are also associated with a longer life. In one study, as the number of organizations volunteered for and the hours of volunteering increased, the likelihood of death during the follow-up period decreased

> Whoever has a bountiful eye will be blessed, for he shares his bread with the poor.
>
> Proverbs 22:9

by 44% reduction for those volunteering for two or more organizations. Interestingly, the effect of volunteering (at any level) on mortality was strongest in those attending religious services at least weekly.[138]

However, just like with church attendance, generosity only affects longevity when it is intrinsic. Only people who are really trying to help others receive the health benefit. People who volunteer appear to live longer as long as their reasons for volunteering are to help others rather than themselves.[139]

d. Serve

Identify your talents and skills. Use them in your church and community. Volunteer a couple of hours a week. Visit people in the hospital or nursing home or those that are homebound. Babysit children to give parents a night out. Give someone a ride to church. Call someone, write someone. Do this once a week and see how it affects you.

Dedicate Yourself

To figure out what you might be good at follow the steps in Romans 12.

> *I appeal to you therefore, brothers, by the mercies of God, to present your bodies as a living sacrifice, holy and acceptable to God, which is your spiritual worship. Do not be conformed to this world, but be transformed by the renewal of your mind, that by testing you may discern what is the will of God, what is good and acceptable and perfect.*
>
> *Romans 12:1-2*

Begin with a decision to offer your life as a life of service. Doing so is a commitment to serve God regardless of your vocation. This is a decision to concentrate on serving rather than being served.

Make a Sober Assessment

> *For by the grace given to me, I say to everyone among you not to think of himself more highly than he ought to think, but to think with sober judgment, each according to the measure of faith that God has assigned.*
>
> *Romans 12:3*

Next, make a sober assessment of your life. What are you good at? What are you not good at? What do you like to do? What do you dislike doing? Identify your gifts. Look for ways you can serve others with them. In Romans 12:5-8, we see examples of gifts God has given people and how they might be used to help others. Use your gifts as an act of worship.

These types of activities have been found to boost moods and result in long-lasting well-being. In one study, the researchers asked students to perform five random acts of kindness per week, over the course of six weeks. Such acts were described as behaviors that benefit others or make others happy, typically at some cost to themselves (e.g., dropping coins into a stranger's parking meter, donating blood, helping a friend with a problem, visiting a sick relative, or writing a thank you note to a former teacher). The group experienced changes in well-being. A control group who did not perform similar acts experienced a decrease in happiness.[140]

e. Give Tithes and Offerings

> Bring the full tithe into the storehouse, that there may be food in my house. And thereby put me to the test, says the Lord of hosts, if I will not open the windows of heaven for you and pour down for you a blessing until there is no more need.
>
> *Malachi 3:10*

Followers of Christ have long practiced tithing. Tithing is to give 10% of ones income while an offering is anything over and above 10%. The Scriptures teach that failure to tithe is to rob

> Each one must give as he has decided in his heart, not reluctantly or under compulsion, for God loves a cheerful giver.
>
> *2 Corinthians 9:7*

God. On the other hand, those who tithe and give offerings are promised blessings. In addition, the Scriptures teach the reason we should seek financial stability is so we might help others. Get yourself into a position so you can give to those in need.

Look for ways to help others. Teach, train, and give. The key is the same; one must give for intrinsic reasons.

> How beautiful upon the mountains are the feet of him who brings good news, who publishes peace, who brings good news of happiness, who publishes salvation, who says to Zion, "Your God reigns."
>
> *Isaiah 52:7*

Tell someone the good news

Finally, you can also give by giving the gospel to others. You might utilize some of the TLCs in this booklet to help others with their health, and help direct them to Christ.

> **Flossing adds 6.4 years to your life.**[141]

7. Be Diligent

The path to better health is tied to being conscientious, diligent, or prudent. When I first read that those who flossed their teeth lived an average of 6.4 years longer than those who did not,

I immediately (after flossing my teeth) thought, "There has got to be something more to that." I suspect they have really measured diligence or prudence.

By the end of the twentieth century, 70% of the Terman men and 51% of the Terman women had died. It was the unconscientious among them that tended to die early. The best predictor of who would live the longest was conscientiousness, prudence, or diligence. Those who had been prudent or dependable as children lived the longest. Why do conscientious people stay healthier and live longer? The researchers noted, they were less likely to engage in dangerous or risky behavior, less likely to smoke, drink excessively, or drive too fast. They were more likely to follow doctor's orders, and enjoy happier marriages.[142]

Can you change?

Perhaps you are thinking, "But I am not conscientious, prudent, or diligent."

People can change. Again, your spiritual life can help here. It appears that religious involvement has a positive impact upon goal selection and self-control (11 out of 12 studies show a positive association). Some suspect that one must engage in prayer and meditation to be capable of creating the neurophysiological changes that are necessary for self-regulation.[143]

Some of the Terman subjects were conscientious early in life but not latter in life and vice versa. It was the ones who scored low on conscientiousness at both points in time that were at the greatest risk for dying. People can change their habits and patterns when they seek out situations that promote responsibility. However, you must enter healthier social environments and relationships to get better.[144]

How do I change?

> *The plans of the diligent lead surely to abundance,*
> *but everyone who is hasty comes only to poverty.*
>
> *Proverbs 21:5*

a. Be Diligent About Relationships

You can begin by working toward success in your relationships. Focus on your immediate family (spouse, parents, children, friends, and coworkers). Select goals that are associated with your family, friends, and that involve harmony and engagement. Avoid goals associated with individuality and personal pleasure.[145]

> *A slack hand causes poverty, but the hand of the diligent makes rich.*
>
> *Proverbs 10:4*

b. Be Prudent About Work

The careless and sloppy among us are not the ones usually chosen to be judges, surgeons, and heads of our most esteemed institutions.

> *He dies for lack of discipline, and because of his great folly he is led astray.*
>
> *Proverbs 5:23*

Today, people are being given rotten advice to slow down, relax, take it easy, and do not work too hard. In the Terman subjects, the responsible and successful achievers thrived in every way, especially if they were dedicated to things and people beyond themselves. One example is Norris Bradbury who is known to have been a Terman subject. He became an atomic physicist who worked on the Manhattan Project and later became the second director of the Los Alamos National Laboratory during the height of the Cold War. He encountered his share of stress and challenges. Yet, he enjoyed a healthy life and lived to the age of 88.

> *The simple believes everything, but the prudent gives thought to his steps.*
>
> *Proverbs 14:15*

The Terman subjects who stayed very involved in meaningful causes and worked the hardest lived the longest. After examining all of the Terman subjects, the researchers classified one-fifth as successful, and one-fifth as unsuccessful. The rest were somewhere in between. Those with the most career success were the least likely to die young. On average, the most successful men lived five years longer than the least successful. The moderately successful lived longer than the less successful, but not as long as the more successful. This is a dose-response relationship—the greater the dose of success, the longer the life.

Ambition, coupled with perseverance, impulse control, and high motivation was not just good for achievement but a package for a resilient work life. A stable and successful career is often key to a successful pathway to long life. The increasing responsibility brings more challenges and a heavier workload, but paradoxically this is helpful to long-term health.[146]

No job requires more responsibility, challenge, and a heavy workload than the presidency of the United States. Some have claimed the stress of the job ages US presidents two years for every year of life in office. This assertion bothered Dr. S. J. Olshansky, a leading researcher in the field of longevity, so he decided to analyze the data. He concluded there was no evidence that US presidents die sooner. On the contrary, 23 of 34 presidents who died of natural causes lived beyond the life expectancy of men of the same age when they were inaugurated.[147]

c. Be Diligent About Health

> The prudent sees danger and hides himself, but the simple go on and suffer for it.
>
> Proverbs 22:3

A significant health downside to optimism involves overlooking or ignoring real threats. This is often called illusory optimism. Optimistic or happy people may underestimate risks to their health and thereby fail to take precautions or to follow medical advice.[148]

The diligent are more likely to take a health problem seriously and cooperate with medical treatment. A Yale University study looked at medication usage after a heart attack. Patients were given either the medication Propranolol or a placebo. Patients who did not cooperate well with their prescribed treatment were more than two times more likely to die within a year of follow-up than patients who took all their pills. The prudent patients were much more likely to survive whether they were on the Propranolol medication or the placebo. It is the overall approach to life that mattered most not the drug.[149] How can you be diligent about your health? You can begin by getting the most out of your medical care. Start with how you communicate with your physician.

Communicate With Your Physician

Often patients feel intimidated in the physician's office. They might disagree with their doctor's diagnosis or medication prescription but are afraid to say so. Yet, it is best to share your opinion and ask questions. Many bad things can happen when communication with the doctor does not work.

Doctor visits are often only ten to fifteen minutes and physicians are increasingly pressed for time. A good relationship with a physician will become more difficult as the health care crisis worsens. Further, more patients will have to see different physicians over time.

Prepare for the Doctor's Visit

You can minimize this problem by preparing for your doctor's visit. Before the visit, write down your questions and concerns. Have a list of topics you wish to discuss.

Stay on Task

Often physicians get behind and are late to appointments. Instead of becoming frustrated and complaining, try to take the view of the busy physician. Stay focused on what you hope to accomplish rather than getting frustrated.

Keep Them Informed

Completely inform your physician of any complementary or alternative medicine practices. These might impact the effect of medications and it is important to keep the physician completely informed.

Follow

Finally, follow your physician's advice. If you disagree with your physician, discuss this with them rather than ignoring their advice.[150]

In peace I will both lie down and sleep; for you alone, O Lord, make me dwell in safety.

Psalm 4:8

---

8. Sleep well

Good health is tied to good sleep. Too little sleep is bad for you, and too much sleep could be worse.[151] Today, Americans sleep less than ever before, and 70 million people experience sleep disorders. Chronic sleep deprivation decreases alertness and impairs judgment, increasing safety risks.[152] It is believed that insomnia affects 10 to 15% of the general population. It is the most prevalent sleep problem.[153] Insufficient sleep is linked to the development of many chronic diseases, such as obesity, heart disease, stroke, depression, and diabetes.[155]

> Insomnia is defined as the inability to initiate or maintain sleep.[154]

In one study, those who woke up more than five times an hour were more likely to have amyloid plaque buildup—a precursor to Alzheimer's disease when compared to those who slept soundly. Those who had trouble going to sleep also had more amyloid plaque in their brains.[156] Even mild chronic sleep deprivation changes brain chemistry and physiology, leading to deterioration of cognition, memory, and mood.[158] Insufficient REM sleep can result in daytime sleepiness, poor concentration, weight gain, and diabetes.[159] Sleep problems can be a vicious cycle.

Major Disasters Documented to be a result of sleep problems

- Exxon Valdez disaster
- Challenger space shuttle explosion
- Three Mile Island nuclear accident
- Chernobyl explosion[157]

Inactivity leads to obesity, which interferes with sleep, which leads to fatigue, which leads to more inactivity. This is a vicious cycle, which left unaddressed can result in major problems. Sustained periods of stress and poor sleep increase levels of cortisol, which in turn leads to loss of cells in the hippocampus area of the brain.[160]

Sleep apnea is a more severe problem that affects millions of Americans. It has been called the "phantom" killer as it is correlated with a higher risk of stroke, heart attack, and sudden death. The chance of death is about one and a half times greater for people with severe sleep disordered breathing compared to people without sleep disordered breathing.[161] Patients with obstructive sleep apnea utilize almost twice as many healthcare resources as those who do not have these difficulties.[162] Sleep apnea increases the risk of hypertension, diabetes, obesity, stroke, cardiovascular disease, and accidents.[163]

> *Amid thoughts from visions of the night,*
> *when deep sleep falls on men.*
>
> *Job 4:13*

What can you do?

While what is a sufficient amount of sleep varies by individual, seven to eight hours a night is usually best.[164] Recent research indicates that today the average adult is sleeping only 6.9 hours per night.[165] There is no evidence on exactly how much sleep we should have.[166]

"Rule of thumb" Guide	
Age	Sleep Needs
School-aged chilren (5 to 12 years)	10.0 to 11.0 hours
Teens (13-17 years)	8.5 to 9.25 hours
Adults	7.0 to 9.0 hours
Older Adults	7.0 to 9.0 hours

How can you know if you are getting the right amount of sleep? If you don't feel refreshed when you wake up, you are not getting the right amount of sleep.[167]

> *If you lie down, you will not be afraid; when*
> *you lie down, your sleep will be sweet.*
>
> *Proverbs 3:24*

a. Develop a Sleep Schedule

There is a lot you can do to improve your sleep if you experience sleep difficulty. Begin by establishing a consistent sleep and wake schedule. Go to bed at the same time and get up at the same time. It is best to maintain this schedule even on holidays and weekends within an hour or two so you will not disrupt your circadian rhythm which governs your sleepiness and wakefulness.[168] It is best to avoid pulling an "all-nighter" to study or work if at all possible.[169] The disruption to your circadian rhythm can take days to correct.

> *Sweet is the sleep of a laborer, whether he eats little or much,*
> *but the full stomach of the rich will not let him sleep.*
>
> *Ecclesiastes 5:12*

b. Prepare for Bed

Formally mark the end of daytime activities and the beginning of evening with relaxing activities.[170] As you prepare to go to bed, develop a relaxing bedtime routine that begins an hour or two before your actual bedtime. Finish eating two to three hours before your regular bedtime. It helps if you have exercised during the day but avoid exercising in the hours before bedtime. Avoid caffeine close to bedtime.[171]

If you have trouble falling asleep, avoid any caffeine after you eat lunch. Avoid bright light in the evening, especially in the hour or two before bed; this includes the light from the television and computers. Avoid arousing activities around bedtime (e. g., heavy study, text messaging, Facebook, and getting into prolonged conversations). Minimize the use of electronic media for about one hour before bedtime.[172] Activities like reading in a quiet room would be more appropriate or listening to calming music which helps to prepare you for bed.

> *At this I awoke and looked, and my sleep was pleasant to me.*
>
> *Jeremiah 31:26*

c. Set up Your Bed

Create an environment that is good to sleep in. Make sure it is dark, comfortable, quiet, and cool. Sleep on a comfortable mattress and pillows. Use your bedroom only for sleep and sex. Avoid watching television, using the computer, or reading in bed. Do not use the bed for work, reading, eating, watching television, or lying awake and worrying. Spend your time in your bed sleeping. Aim to fall asleep within 10 to 20 minutes after going to bed and rise within 10-20 minutes of waking up in the morning.

d. In Bed

One myth about sleep is that it is normal to fall asleep almost immediately after going to bed and sleeping through the night without waking.[173] If you can't sleep, tell yourself, "resting without sleep is still good rest; I don't need eight hours of sleep to function." If you can't go to sleep, after 30 minutes get up, listen to quiet music for 30 minutes or until sleepy. Go to another room, with soft light and read or listen to music.[174]

e. Getting Up

Expose yourself to bright morning light or very bright artificial light indoors during morning hours to help regulate circadian rhythms.[175] See your primary care physician if you have prolonged sleep problems to rule out basic health concerns and seek clearance for exercise.

9. Be Physically Active

Regular physical activity:

Reduces the risk of dying prematurely.
Reduces of the risk of dying prematurely from heart disease.
Reduces the risk of developing diabetes.
Reduces the risk of developing high blood pressure.
Reduces the risk of developing colon cancers.
Reduces feelings of depression and anxiety.
Helps control weight.
Helps reduce blood pressure in people who already have high blood pressure.
Helps build and maintain healthy bones, muscles, and joints.
Helps older adults become strong and better and to move about without falling.
Promotes psychological well-being.[176]

Good health involves being active. Sedentary people have nearly twice the risk of heart disease as those involved in high intensity exercise.[177]

According to a meta-analysis of 38 studies on mortality and physical activity of women, those who were the most physically active were 34% less likely to die during follow-up when compared to those who were the least active.[178] In other studies, men who were physically fit had a 44% lower mortality rate than unfit men, with the likelihood of death being reduced by 8% for every extra minute of maximum time spent on the treadmill.[179]

In a twelve-year follow-up study of 1,700 cases where coronary heart disease (CHD) had been identified, men who ran an hour a week or more had a 42% reduction in risk for CHD. Those who trained with weights for thirty minutes a week or more had a 23% reduction; those who rowed for one hour a week or more had an 18% reduction; and those who walked briskly for thirty minutes a day or more had an 18% reduction. Both duration and intensity of exercise was associated with reduced CHD risk. Among those who already have CHD, physical inactivity nearly doubles the risk of future coronary events.[180] Compared to no exercise, physical activity predicted a nearly 50% reduction in risk of cognitive impairment, Alzheimer's disease, and other dementias in one study.[181]

Exercise has been suggested as a strategy to improve sleep quality, cognitive performance in older age, and in reducing job burnout.[182] Physical activity is good medicine.

> *For while bodily training is of some value, godliness is of value in every way, as it holds promise for the present life and also for the life to come.*
>
> *1 Timothy 4:8*

Is it too late?

If you are inactive, you can increase your activity and improve your health. In the Terman subjects, those who were inactive in youth and became more active later in life often did almost as well in terms of lifespan as those who were active their entire lives.

Start Slowly

Yet, 25% of the U.S. population report zero leisure time and physical activity. Why are so few physically active even though we know it would benefit us? It may be that many start out exercising too hard. So start slowly. People are more likely to quit exercising when they exceed their respiration threshold. The respiration threshold is the point when it gets hard to talk when exercising. The motive for exercising is important as well. It seems that those who exercise to lose weight or lower cholesterol are often discouraged because it usually takes months to see those kinds of results. Instead, exercise to improve your mood. Make a point to exercise when you feel down, just as you might take an aspirin when you have a headache.[183]

> "I desire now to repeat and emphasize that maxim:
> We can't reach old age by another's road. My habits
> protect my life, but they would assassinate you."
>
> Mark Twain

Do what you enjoy

Perhaps one impediment to becoming physically active is the fear that one must begin a life as a jogger. If you jog an hour almost every day over a year, you will spend about 360 hours doing this. If you jog for 40 years (say, from age twenty-one to age sixty-one), you will spend about 14,400 hours jogging. Assuming that most of us are awake for about 16 hours a day, this means you would be spending the equivalent of about 900 days jogging. Friedman and Martin (2011) noted that this would be about two and a half years spent exercising. That is a long time to spend jogging if you do not enjoy it.

Jogging is a recent social phenomenon, and many Terman participants remained steadily active in a healthy way having never seen or heard of a jogging trail. There are many ways to be physically active: jogging, swimming, bicycling, walking, mowing the lawn, playing a musical instrument, vacuuming, playing tennis, walking the dog, and anything else that gets you up and moving.

Choose activities you enjoy and spend thirty minutes at least four times per week doing. Your job may not allow you to swim for 30 minutes, four times a week. So, it is more likely you will do some combination of these. Do something you really enjoy, that will benefit your body and your soul. Do whatever you want to do that gets you out of your chair at least 20-30 minutes a day.[184] The activity need not be strenuous. Heavy exercise has no benefits beyond moderate exercise.[185] It is physical inactivity that is a predictor of earlier death.[186] So use the chart below to develop your own activities to get active.

	Ran	Walked	Biked	Swam	Tennis	Mowed	Gardened	Other
Weekly Activity Log								
S								
M	20							
T								Basketball-60
W		25						
Th		20						
F						60		
SA			120				60	

* of minutes

10. Eat a proper diet.

A booklet on health would not be complete without a look at diet. Indeed, eating a healthy diet is a key TLC. Physical activity alone will not lead to good health if you eat an unhealthy diet. For example, to burn off the amount of calories ingested when eating a *Big Mac* one would have to run for 45 minutes, cycle or swim for 60 minutes, or walk for 90 minutes.[187] Diet must be addressed. Unfortunately, not every relationship between health and religious involvement is positive. In 86% of the studies on religion and health, being religious has been associated with greater weight. Since greater weight has severe consequences this is a critical TLC to address.

Those who are overweight have a 73% increased risk of hypertension and those who are obese have a 339% increased risk.[188] As we have already discussed, obesity is now viewed as the number two cause of death, following only smoking. Obesity is linked to most diseases, for example being overweight or obese is a contributing factor in 14 to 20% of all cancer-related deaths.[189] So how can we get started on a healthier diet?

> *For the drunkard and the glutton will come to poverty,*
> *and slumber will clothe them with rags.*
>
> *Proverbs 23:21*

What can we do to eat healthier?

a. Don't Eat Too Much

We can begin by simply not eating too much. It is important to monitor how and what we eat. The work of Dr. Jean Kristeller, co-founder of The Center for Mindful Eating, states simply, "Eat when you are hungry, stop when you're full." She has developed an intervention called Mindfulness Based Eating Awareness Training (MB-EAT) which we will now briefly describe.

> *It is not good to eat much honey . . .*
>
> *Proverbs 25:27a*
>
> *And put a knife to your throat if you are given to appetite.*
>
> *Proverbs 23:2*

Avoid Mindless Eating

Avoid mindless eating when watching television, surfing the Internet, or reading the newspaper. Be aware of your hunger and eat only when hunger appears. The goal is to stop eating simply because you have been triggered to do so by a commercial or eating when bored or depressed.

Savor the Taste

Once you begin to eat, chew food slowly and tune into the taste. Our taste buds tire quickly, so the first bites of food taste better than later ones. After eating a large amount of food, there may be no taste experienced at all. The key is to focus on the quality of food rather than quantity. Do not be discouraged when you occasionally overeat. In one study using Kristeller's approach, those who struggled with binge eating were able to reduce bingeing from four times a week to one. In a study with obese women, they saw a reduction in anxiety, chronic stress, and belly fat after utilizing this approach.[190]

b. Address the Cues

You can better avoid mindless eating by addressing the cues or triggers to eat by making simple changes in your pantry like moving bran cereal to the front and Pop Tarts to the back. Use smaller plates and glasses which tends to result in eating less food. How we think about food triggers our appetite as well. For example, people report that food tastes better when a dish is called "succulent Italian seafood filet" instead of "seafood filet." So watch and perhaps rethink your thoughts about healthier food.[191]

c. Eat Breakfast

Eating breakfast will help you have a healthy weight. In one study, obese, non-diabetic adults were examined. They ate breakfast and even added dessert to their breakfast (e.g., cookies, cake, chocolate). On average, they lost 40 pounds more than a group who avoided such foods. A morning meal staves off cravings and defuses psychological cravings to sweet foods.[192]

d. Write Down What You Eat

In a study of overweight women who participated in a weight-loss program, the results indicated that those who kept a food journal lost an average of six pounds more than those who did not. The more detailed the journal the more effective it was.[193] We tend to eat more food and less healthy food than we think. Monitoring your food intake by making a diagram like the one below can help you make sure you are not eating too much and that you are eating enough key foods.

	Breakfast	Lunch	Dinner	Snacks
S				
M				
T				
W				
Th				
F				
Sa				
Goal:				

* Daily: Fruit, nuts, non-fried vegetables (not including potatoes)
** Weekly: Fish (nonfried), salmon or tuna preferred

e. Lighten Up

Even modest weight loss has benefits. In a study of over 3,000 overweight people over ten years, even a small weight loss (average of 14 pounds) reduced the risk of Type-2 diabetes by 58%. These benefits remained up to ten years even if they regained their weight.

What to Eat

Try a Mediterranean type diet. There is a 20% reduction in all-cause mortality among those who eat a Mediterranean type diet. The diet is high in vegetables (excluding potatoes), fruit and nuts, whole grains, fish, monounsaturated fat, and low in dairy and meat products.[194]

> Adherence to a Mediterranean type diet (high in vegetables, fruits, legumes, cereals, low intake of saturated fat, moderate fish intake, low meat and poultry intake) predicts a slowing in cognitive decline with aging.[195]

A Mediterranean style diet protects against blood vessel damage in the brain, reducing the risks of stroke and memory loss.[196] A key component to the diet is omega-3 fatty acid (or fish) consumption which is associated with lower risk of heart problems.[197]

> The DASH diet (Dietary Approaches to Stop Hypertension) calls for eating more fruits, vegetables, and low-fat dairy products, fish, poultry, and nuts; eating less meat and sweets; and eating foods rich in magnesium, potassium, and calcium.[198]

Replace unhealthy snacks with the consumption of nuts. Nuts have also been found to reduce heart disease.[199] Try to eat fruit and vegetables as often as you can, which also reduce the risk of heart disease and reduce the risk of morbidity and mortality.[200] All of these foods have been found to reduce blood pressure as well.

When considering a diet high in fish and vegetables, many complain that healthy foods are more expensive than non-healthy. However, a closer look does not indicate that to be the case. Perhaps buying fresh salmon or tuna in a supermarket would be more expensive than buying certain meats. However, the same nutritional value is obtained from canned tuna or salmon. Similarly, though fresh vegetables and fruit might seem to be more expensive than high fat content fast food, this may not be the case when one considers canned vegetables or canned fruit. Further, it is important to view food as an investment, even though one might be paying somewhat more for healthy food today. Eventually, the cost can pay off in fewer physician and prescription co-payments and out of pocket medical expenses.

Lay off the salt

A decrease in salt intake (by nearly one-third) took place in Finland over thirty years. It was found to be an important factor in the decline in average blood pressure and a 75-80% decline in stroke and coronary heart disease mortality of Fins under age sixty-five. As a result of this data, many have suggested limiting sodium intake to 1,500 mg per day (about two-thirds of a teaspoon, which includes both added salt and salt in processed foods ingested) to greatly enhance health.[201]

Conclusion

I encourage you to make these 10 TLCs to your life. Perhaps it is time we began to view developing good health as an issue of stewardship. If you are a follower of Christ your body is the "temple of the Holy Spirit" so it is important to take care of it. Doing so increases your capability of ministering to others.

Consider the parable of the talents (Matthew 25:14-30). One was given five talents and another only one. Look at the parable from the perspective of good and bad health. If you have been blessed with good health, consider the opportunities you have that the less healthy do not have. Consider how maintaining good health puts you into a position to serve rather than being served. If you have bad health, the parable puts your position in perspective. We are called to simply use what we have to the best of our ability. Let us go forth and practice these TLCs. All of them are founded upon Scripture and lead to not only better physical health, but better spiritual, social, and psychological health as well.

Beloved, I pray that all may go well with
you and that you may be in good health,
as it goes well with your soul.
3 John 1:2

References

[1] S. Czekalinski. U.S. Birth Rate Hits Record Low. *National Journal.* Accessed January 9, 2013 at http://www.nationaljournal.com/thenextamerica/demographics/u-s-birth-rate-hits-record-low-20121129. (November 29, 2012).

[2] American Cancer Society and R. V. Snowden. ACOG revises cervical cancer screening guidelines. Accessed January 9, 2013 at http://www.cancer.org/cancer/news/news/acog-revises-cervical-cancer-screening-guidelines. (November 20, 2009).

[3] A. Jemal, et al. Annual Report to the nation on the status of cancer, 1975-2005, featuring trends in lung cancer, tobacco use, and tobacco control. *Journal of the National Cancer Institute, 100* (23):1672-1694. (2008).

[4] D. Lloyd-Jones, et al. Heart disease and stroke statistics—2009 update: A report from the American Heart Association Statistics Committee and Stroke Statistics Subcommittee. *Circulation, 119*:e21-e181. Accessed on December 12, 2012 at http://circ.ahajournals.org/content/119/3/e21.full.pdf. (2009).

[5] J. Lloyd. Soaring knee surgeries put strain on budgets. *USA Today* (Page 1) (September 26, 2012).

[6] S. Czekalinski. (November 29, 2012).

[7] National Heart, Lung, and Blood Institute. Disease Statistics, Chapter 4. *NHLBI Fact Book Fiscal Year 2011,* Bethesda, MD: National Institutes of Health. Accessed on December 12, 2012 at http://www.nhlbi.nih.gov/about/factbook/chapter4.htm. (2011).

[8] D. Lloyd-Jones., et al. (2009).

[9] American Heart Association. *Heart Disease and Stroke Statistics—2013 Update.* Accessed January 1, 2013 at http://circ.ahajournals.org/content/127/1/e6.full.pdf+html. (2013).

[10] A. Wayne. Doctor shortage may swell to 130,000 with cap. *Bloomberg.* Accessed December 13, 2012 at http://www.bloomberg.com/news/2012-08-29/doctor-shortage-may-swell-to-130-000-with-u-s-cap.html. (August 29, 2012).

[11] H. G. Koenig and D. M. Lawson. *Faith in the Future: Healthcare, Aging, and the Role of Religion.* Philadelphia and London: Templeton Foundation Press. (2007).

[12] Centers for Disease Control and Prevention. *Life Expectancy.* Accessed December 26, 2012 at http://www.cdc.gov/nchs/fastats/lifexpec.htm. (2009).

13 Centers for Disease Control and Prevention. *Cholesterol: Facts.* Accessed September 2, 2012. http://www.cdc.gov/cholesterol/facts.htm. Surgeon General Report. 2010. *The Surgeon General's Vision for a Healthy and Fit Nation.* Assessed September 2, 2012. http://www.surgeongeneral.gov/library/obesityvision/index.html. (2010).

14 S. Bennett Johnson. President's Column: Addressing the obesity epidemic: Don't blame the victim. *Monitor on Psychology, 43* (9):5. (October 2012).

15 M. Machione. Strokes on the rise among young and middle aged Americans. *The Washington Post (A Section).* (February 10, 2011).

16 K. L. Ong, et al. Prevalence, awareness, treatment, and control of hypertension among United States adults 1999-2004. *Hypertension, 49* (1):69-75 (2007).

17 S. E. Straus, et al. New evidence for stroke prevention: Scientific review. *Journal of the American Medical Association, 288:*1388-1395. (2002).

18 Centers for Disease Control and Prevention. (2010).

19 S. E. Straus, et al. (2002).

20 E. Glicksman. Preparing for the "Silver Tsunami." *Monitor on Psychology, 43* (9): 32-35. (October 2012).

21 S. Martin. Our health at risk. *Monitor on Psychology, 43* (3):18. (March 2012).

22 H. S. Friedman and L. R. Martin. *The longevity project: Surprising discoveries for health and long life from the landmark eight-decade study.* New York: Hudson Street Press. (2011).

23 American Heart Association/American Stroke Association. *Understanding risk.* Accessed on December 26, 2012 at http://www.strokeassociation.org/STROKEORG/AboutStroke/UnderstandingRisk/Understanding-Stroke-Risk_UCM_308539_SubHomePage.jsp. (2012).

24 E. Glicksman. (October 2012).

25 C. DeCarli. Mild cognitive impairment: Prevalence, prognosis, aetiology, and treatment. *Lancet Neurology, 2:*15. (2003).

26 D. Vaidya, et al. Incidence of coronary artery disease in siblings of patients with premature coronary artery disease: 10 years of follow-up. *American Journal of Cardiology, 100* (9):1410-1415. (2007).

27 K. Jood, et al. Family history in ischemic stroke before 70 years of age. *Stroke, 36:*1383-1387. (2005).

28 K. Christensen, et al. The quest for genetic determinants of human longevity: Challenges and insights. *National Reviews: Genetics, 7:*436-448. (2006).

29 V. Hjelmborg, et al. Genetic influence on human lifespan and longevity. *Human Genetics, 119* (3):312-321. (2006).

30 A. J. Midei, et al. Childhood physical abuse is associated with incident metabolic syndrome in mid-life women. *Health Psychology.* Advance online publication. doi:10.1037/a0027891. (July 9, 2012).

31 C. S. Widom, et al. A prospective investigation of physical health outcomes in abused and neglected children: New findings from a 30-Year follow-up. *American Journal of Public Health, 102* (6):1135-1144. (2012).

[32] National Cancer Institute. *What You Need to Know about Cancer: Screening.* Accessed December 28, 2012 at http://www.cancer.gov/cancertopics/wyntk/overview/page4. (2006).

[33] World Health Organization. *The World Health Report 2008, Primary Health Care: Now More than Ever.* Accessed December 28, 2012. http://www.who.int/whr/2008/whr08_en.pdf. (2008).

National Center for Health Statistics (2005). *Deaths and mortality.* Atlanta, GA: Centers for Disease Control, Accessed December 28, 2012. http://www.cdc.gov/nchs/FASTATS/deaths.htm. (2011).

[34] H. K. Neilson, et al. Physical activity and postmenopausal breast cancer: Proposed biologic mechanisms and areas for future research. *Cancer Epidemiology, Biomarkers and Prevention, 18* (1): 11-27. (2009).

[35] E. Linos, et al. Diet and breast cancer. *Current Oncology Reports, 9* (1):31-41. (2007).

[36] Centers for Disease Control and Prevention. FastStats: Accidents or Unintentional Injuries. Accessed December 26, 2012 at http://www.cdc.gov/nchs/fastats/acc-inj.htm. (2009).

[37] American Cancer Society. *Cancer Facts and Figures 2012.* Accessed December 29, 2012 at http://www.cancer.org/acs/groups/content/@epidemiologysurveilance/documents/document/acspc-031941.pdf. (2012).

[38] E. Linos, et al. (2007).

[39] A. H. Mokdad, et al. Actual causes of death in the United States, 2000. *Journal of the American Medical Association, 291:*1238-1245. (2004).

[40] H. G. Koenig. *Medicine, Religion, and Health: Where Science and Spirituality Meet.* West Conshohocken, PA: Templeton Foundation Press. (2008).

[41] G. N. Armaiz-Pena, et al. Neuroendocrine modulation of cancer progression. *Brain, Behavior, and Immunity, 23:*10-15. (2009).

[42] J. Chamberlin. Protecting your aging brain. *Monitor on Psychology, 42* (9):48-49. (October 2011).

[43] E. Glicksman. (October 2012).

[44] D. Lloyd-Jones, et al. (2009).

[45] F. J. He and G. A. MacGregor. Cost of poor pressure control in the UK: 62,000 unnecessary deaths per year. *Journal of Human Hypertension, 17:*455-457. (2003).

[46] M. Briel, et al. Association between change in high density lipoprotein cholesterol and cardiovascular disease morbidity and mortality: Systematic review and meta-regression analysis. *British Medical Journal, 338:b92.* (2009).

[47] R. Walsh. Lifestyle and Mental Health, *American Psychologist, 66* (7):579-592. (2011).

[48] H. S. Friedman and L. R. Martin. (2011).

[49] M. E. McCullough, et al. Religious involvement and mortality: A meta-analytic review. *Health Psychology, 19* (3):211-222. (2000).

[50] H. G. Koenig. (2008).

[51] The Pew Research Center. Religion Among the Millennials. Accessed December 5, 2012. http://www.pewforum.org/uploadedFiles/Topics/Demographics/Age/millennials-report.pdf. (February 2010).

[52] R. A. Hummer, et al. Religious involvement and U.S. adult mortality. *Demography, 36*:273-285. (1999).

[53] J. S. Levin, et al. Religious effects on health status and life satisfaction among black Americans. The *Journals of Gerontology Series B: Psychological Sciences Social Sciences, 50B*:S154-S63. (1995).

[54] R. A. Hummer, et al. (1999).

[55] R. A. Hummer, et al. (1999).

[56] W. J. Strawbridge, et al. Frequent attendance at religious services and mortality over twenty-eight years. *American Journal of Public Health, 87*:957-961. (1997).

[57] H. G. Koenig, et al. Does religious attendance prolong survival?: A six-year follow-up study of 3,968 adults. *The Journals of Gerontology Series A: Biological Sciences and Medical Sciences. 54A*:M370-377. (1999).

[58] H. G. Koenig. (2008).

[59] H. G. Koenig. (2008).

[60] H. G. Koenig. *The Healing Power of Faith: Science Explores Medicine's Last Great Frontier.* New York: Simon & Schuster. (1999).

[61] M. McCullough. Religious Involvement and Mortality: Answers and More Questions. *Faith and Health: Psychological Perspectives* (Eds. T. G. Plante and A. C. Sherman). New York: The Guilford Press. (2001).

[62] H. G. Koenig. (2008).

[63] J. E. Yonker. *Religious service attendance in older adults: Predictors and cognitive outcomes.* Unpublished manuscript. (2010).

[64] E. L. Idler and S. V. Kasl. Religion among disabled and nondisabled elderly persons, II: Attendance at religious services as a predictor of the course of disability. *The Journals of Gerontology Series B: Psychological Sciences and Social Sciences, 52B*:S306-S316. (1997).

[65] H. G. Koenig. (2008).

[66] M. McCullough. (2001).

[67] A. Ellis. The advantages and disadvantages of self-help therapy materials. *Professional Psychology: Research and Practice, 24* (3):335-339. (1993).

[68] H. Helms, et al. Effects of private religious activity on mortality of elderly disabled and nondisabled adults. *The Journals of Gerontology Series A: Biological Sciences and Medical Sciences, 55A*:M400-M405. (2000).

[69] H. G. Koenig, et al. The relationship between religious activities and blood pressure in older adults. *International Journal of Psychiatry in Medicine, 28*:189-213. (1998).

[70] P. A. Boyle, et al. Effect of a purpose in life on risk of incident Alzheimer disease and mild cognitive impairment in community-dwelling older persons. *Archives of General Psychiatry, 67*:304-310. (2010).

[71] H. G. Koenig, et al. *Handbook of Religion and Health—Second Edition.* Oxford: Oxford University Press. (2012).

[72] S. K. Lutgendorf, et al. Sense of coherence moderates the relationship between life stress and natural killer cell activity in healthy older adults. *Psychology and Aging, 14:*552-563. (1999).

[73] A. Keller, et al. Does the perception that stress affects health matter? The association with health and mortality. *Health Psychology, 31:*677-684. (2012).

[74] B. J. Shen, et al. Anxiety characteristics independently and prospectively predict myocardial infarction in men. The unique contribution of anxiety among psychological factors. *Journal of the American College of Cardiology, 51:*113-119. (2008).

[75] J. Denollet, et al. Anxiety predicted premature all-cause and cardiovascular death in a 10-year follow-up of middle-aged women. *Journal of Clinical Epidemiology, 62:*452-456. (2009).

[76] H. G. Koenig. (2008).

[77] A. Keller, et al. (2012).

[78] H. S. Friedman and L. R. Martin. (2011).

[79] H. G. Koenig. *Spirituality in Patient Care: Why, How, When, and What.* Philadelphia and London: Templeton Foundation Press. (2002).

[80] K. I. Pargament, et al. Religious struggle as a predictor of mortality among medically ill elderly patients: A two-year longitudinal study. *Archives of Internal Medicine, 161:*1881-1885. (August 13, 2001).

[81] H. G. Koenig. (1999).

[82] L. F. Berkman and S. L. Syme. Social networks, host resistance, and mortality: A nine year follow-up study of Alameda County residents. *American Journal of Epidemiology, 109:*186-204. (1979).

[83] H. G. Koenig. (2008).

[84] D. S. Strogatz, et al. Social support, stress, and blood pressure in black adults. *Epidemiology, 8* (5):482-487. (1997).

D. S. Strogatz and S. A. James. Social support and hypertension among blacks and whites in a rural, southern community. *American Journal of Epidemiology, 124*(6):949-956. (1986).

[85] A. Shankar, et al. Loneliness, social isolation, and behavioral and biological health indicators in older adults. *Health Psychology.* Advance online publication. Doi: 10.1037/a0022826. (2011).

[86] H. G. Koenig. (2008).

[87] M. M. Burg, et al. Low perceived social support and post-myocardial infarction prognosis in the Enhancing Recovery in Coronary Heart Disease clinical trial: The effects of treatments. *Psychosomatic Medicine, 67:*879-888. (2005).

[88] D. Spiegel, et al. Effects of supportive-expressive group therapy on survival of patients with metastatic breast cancer. *Lancet, 2:*(8668): 888-891. (1989).

[89] H. G. Koenig. (2008).

[90] B. Nausheen, et al. Social support and cancer progression: A systematic review. *Journal of Psychosomatic Research, 67:*403-415. (2009).

[91] H. S. Friedman and L. R. Martin. (2011).

[92] G. E. Vaillant. *Aging Well: Surprising Guideposts to a Happier Life from the Landmark Harvard Study of Adult Development.* Boston: Little, Brown, and Co. (2002).

[93] K. B. King and H. T. Reis. Marriage and long-term survival after coronary artery bypass grafting. *Health Psychology, 31:*55-62. (2012).

[94] H. G. Koenig. (2008).

[95] D. A. Reinhard, et al. Expensive egos: Narcissistic males have higher cortisol. *PLoS ONE 7*(1): e30858. doi:10.1371/journal.pone.0030858. (2012).

[96] D. S. Strogatz, et al. (1997).

D. S. Strogatz and S. A. James. (1986).

[97] B. Baker, et al. Marital support, spousal contact and the course of mild hypertension. *Journal of Psychosomatic Research, 55*(3):229-233. (2003).

[98] C. C. Guimont, et al. Effects of job strain on blood pressure: A prospective study of male and female white-collar workers. *American Journal of Public Health, 96* (8):1436-1443. (2006).

[99] S. E. Taylor and D. K. Sherman. Positive Psychology and Health Psychology: A Fruitful Liaison. P. A. Linley & S. Joseph (Eds) In *Positive Psychology in Practice* (pp. 305-319). Hoboken, New Jersey: John Wiley & Sons, Inc. (2004).

[100] D. E. Bradley. Religious involvement and social resources: Evidence from the data set "Americans' Changing Lives." *Journal for the Scientific Study of Religion, 34:*259-267. (1995).

[101] R. De Vogli, et al. Negative aspects of close relationships and heart disease. *Archives of Internal Medicine, 167:*1951-197. (2007).

[102] N. Krause and J. Cairney. Close companion friends in church and health in late life. *Review of Religious Research, 51* (2):181-200. (2009).

[103] A. Novotney. Money can't buy happiness with Dr. Robert Kenny. *Monitor on Psychology, 43* (7):25-27. (2012).

[104] P. E. Anderson. *The Powerful Bond between People and Pets: Our boundless connections to companion animals.* Westport, CT: Praeger. (2008).

[105] H. S. Friedman and L. R. Martin. (2011).

[106] L. Toussaint, et al. Forgive to live: Forgiveness, Health, and Longevity. *Journal of Behavioral Medicine, 35* (4):375-386. (2012).

[107] E. L. Worthington, et al. Unforgiveness, forgiveness, religion, and health. *In Faith and Health: Psychological Perspectives* (Eds. T. G. Plante, & A. C. Sherman). New York: The Guilford Press. (2001).

[108] H. G. Koenig. (2008).

[109] J. K. Kiecolt-Glaser, et al. Negative behavior during marital conflict is associated with immunological down-regulation. *Psychosomatic Medicine, 55:*395-409. (1993).

[110] H. G. Koenig. *Chronic Pain: Biomedical and Spiritual Approaches.* New York, London, Oxford: The Haworth Pastoral Press. (2003).

[111] M. A. Waltman, et al. The effects of a forgiveness intervention on patients with coronary artery disease. *Psychology and Health, 24* (1):11-27. (2009).

[112] G. Bono and M. E. McCullough. Positive responses to benefit and harm: Bringing forgiveness and gratitude into cognitive psychotherapy. *Journal of Cognitive Psychotherapy: An International Quarterly, 20* (2):147-158. (2006). M. E. McCullough, et al. Writing about the benefits of an interpersonal transgression facilitates forgiveness. *Journal of Consulting and Clinical Psychology, 74* (5):887-897. (2006).

[113] H. S. Friedman and L. R. Martin. (2011).

[114] M. E. McCullough. Forgiveness: Who does it and how do they do it? *Current Directions in Psychological Science, 10* (6):194-197. (2001). G. Bono and M. E. McCullough. (2006).

[115] H. S. Friedman and L. R. Martin. (2011).

[116] M. E. McCullough. (2001). And G. Bono and M. E. McCullough. (2006).

[117] M. E. McCullough. (2001). And G. Bono and M. E. McCullough. (2006).

[118] M. E. McCullough. (2001). And G. Bono and M. E. McCullough. (2006).

[119] S. C. Segerstrom. Optimism and immunity: Do positive thoughts always lead to positive effects. *Brain, Behavior, and Immunity, 19*:195-200. (2005).

[120] D. Watson and K. Naragon. Positive Affectivity: The Disposition to Experience Positive Emotional States. S. J. Lopez and C. R. Snyder (Eds.) In *Oxford Handbook of Positive Psychology* (pp. 207-215). Oxford: Oxford University Press. (2009).

[121] H. S. Friedman and L. R. Martin. (2011).

[122] H. A. Tindle, et al. Optimism, cynical hostility, and incident coronary heart disease and mortality in the women's health initiative. *Circulation, 120*:656-662. (2009).

[123] B. K. Gorman and A. Sivaganesan. The role of social support and integration for understanding socioeconomic disparities in self-rated health and hypertension. *Social Science and Medicine, 65* (5):958-975. (2007).

[124] T. M. Pollard and J. E. Schwartz. Are changes in blood pressure and total cholesterol related to changes in mood? An 18-month study of men and women. *Health Psychology, 22* (1):47-53. (2003).

[125] R. G. Jacob, et al. Ambulatory blood pressure responses and the circumplex model of mood: A 4-day study. *Psychosomatic Medicine, 61* (3):319-333. (1999).

[126] UC Irvine Today. Email "vacations" decrease stress, increase concentration. Accessed September 1, 2012 at http://today.uci.edu/news/2012/05/nr_email_120503.php. (2012).

[127] B. Schwartz. *The Paradox of Choice: Why More is Less, How the Culture of Abundance Robs Us of Satisfaction.* New York: Harper Collins. (2004).

[128] G. K. Chesterson. *A short history of England.* London: William Clowes & Sons. (1917).

[129] P. C. Watkins, et al. Furthering the Science of Gratitude. S. J. Lopez and C. R. Snyder (Eds.) In *Oxford Handbook of Positive Psychology* (pp. 437-445). Oxford: Oxford University Press. (2009).

[130] R. McCraty and D. Childre. The Grateful Heart: The Psychophysiology of Appreciation. R. A. Emmons and M. E. McCullough (Eds.) In *The Psychology of Gratitude* (pp. 230-255). New York: Oxford University Press. (2004).

[131] G. Alspach. Extending the tradition of giving thanks: Recognizing the health benefits of gratitude. *Critical Care Nurse, 26* (6):12-18. (2009).

[132] S. Lyubomirsky, et al. *Pursuing sustained happiness through random acts of kindness and counting one's blessings: Tests of two six-week interventions.* Unpublished data. University of California, Riverside. Department of Psychology. (2004).

[133] R. A. Emmons and M. E. McCullough. Counting blessings versus burdens: An experimental investigation of gratitude and subjective well-being in daily life. *Journal of Personality and Social Psychology, 84*:377-389. (2003).

[134] K. M. Sheldon and S. Lyubomirsky. Achieving sustainable new happiness: Prospects, practices, and prescriptions. P. A. Linley and S. Joseph (Eds.) In *Positive Psychology in Practice* (pp. 127-145). Hoboken, NJ: John Wiley & Sons. (2004).

[135] S. C. Lechner, et al. Benefit-Finding and Growth. S. J. Lopez and C. R. Snyder (Eds.) In *Oxford Handbook of Positive Psychology* (pp. 633-640), Oxford: Oxford University Press. (2009).

[136] H. G. Koenig. (2008).

[137] C. D. Batson, et al. Empathy and Altruism. S. J. Lopez & C. R. Snyder (Eds.) In *Oxford Handbook of Positive Psychology* (pp. 417-426). Oxford: Oxford University Press. (2009).

[138] D. Oman, et al. Volunteerism and mortality among the community-dwelling elderly. *Journal of Health Psychology, 4*:301-316. (1999).

[139] S. Konrath, et al. Motives for volunteering are associated with mortality risk in older adults. *Health Psychology, 31* (1):87-96. (2011).

[140] K. M. Sheldon and S. Lyubomirsky. Achieving sustainable new happiness. (2004).

[141] M. R. Roizen. *The Real Age Makeover: Take years off your looks and add them to your life.* New York: Harper Collins. (2004).

[142] H. S. Friedman and L. R. Martin. (2011).

[143] M. E. McCullough and B. L. B. Willoughby. Religion, Self-Regulation, and Self-Control: Associations, Explanations, and Implications. *Psychological Bulletin, 135* (1): 69-93. (2009).

[144] H. S. Friedman and L. R. Martin. (2011).

[145] M. E. McCullough and B. L. B. Willoughby. (2009).

[146] H. S. Friedman and L. R. Martin. (2011).

[147] S. J. Olshansky. Aging of US Presidents. *Journal of the American Medical Association, 306* (21):2328-2329. (2011).

[148] H. S. Friedman and L. R. Martin. (2011).

[149] R. I. Horwitz, et al. Treatment Adherence and Risk of Death after a Myocardial Infarction. *Lancet, 336* (8714):542-545. (1990).

[150] K. Weir. Improving patient-physician communication. *Monitor on Psychology, 43* (10):36-40. (2012).

[151] M. A. Grandner and N. P. Patel. From sleep duration to mortality: implications of meta-analysis and future directions. *Journal of Sleep Research, 18*:145-147. (2009).

[152] M. E. Wells and B. V. Vaughn. Poor sleep challenging the health of a nation. *The Neurodiagnostic Journal, 53*:233-249. (2012).

[153] C. Drake, et al. Vulnerability to stress-related sleep disturbance and hyperarousal. *Sleep, 27*:285-291. (2004).

[154] J. D. Edinger and M. K. Means. Overview of insomnia: definitions, epidemiology, differential diagnosis, and assessment. M. H. Kryger, T. Roth, W. C. Dement (Eds). In *Principles and Practice of Sleep Medicine. Fourth Edition.* Philadelphia: Elsevier Saunders. (2005).

[155] T. J. Balkin, et al. Sleep Loss and Sleepiness: Current Issues. *Chest, 134*:653-660. (2008).

Centers for Disease Control and Prevention. Sleep and chronic disease. Accessed on November 30, 2012 at http://www.cdc.gov/sleep/about_sleep/chronic_disease.htm. (2012).

[156] A. Novotney. Proactive Good Sleep Hygiene. *Monitor on Psychology, 43* (5):16. (2012).

[157] M. E. Wells and B. V. Vaughn. (2012).

[158] National Institute of Neurological Disorders and Stroke. *Brain Basics: Understanding Sleep.* Accessed on January 1, 2013 at http://www.ninds.nih.gov/disorders/brain_basics/understanding_sleep.htm. (2007).

[159] S. S. Holcomb. Putting insomnia to rest. *The Nurse Practitioner, 32* (4):28-34. (2007).

D. E. Watenpaugh. The role of sleep dysfunction in physical inactivity and its relationship to obesity. *Current Sports Medicine Reports, 8*:331-338. (2009).

[160] F. H. Gage. Mammalian neural stem cells. *Science, 287*:1433-1438. (2000).

[161] N. M. Punjabi, et al. Sleep-disordered breathing and mortality: a prospective cohort study. *PLoS Med* 6e 1000132. (2009).

[162] M. E. Wells and B. V. Vaughn. (2012).

[163] T. Young, et al. Sleep disordered breathing and mortality: eighteen-year follow-up of the Wisconsin sleep cohort. *Sleep, 31*:1071-1078. (2008).

[164] National Institute of Neurological Disorders and Stroke. (2007).

[165] National Sleep Foundation. 2005 Adult sleep habits and styles. 2005 Sleep in America poll. Accessed January 1, 2013 at http://www.sleepfoundation.org/article/sleep-america-polls/2005-adult-sleep-habits-and-styles. (2005).

[166] National Sleep Foundation. (2005).

[167] M. E. Wells and B. V. Vaughn. (2012).

[168] M. E. Wells and B. V. Vaughn. (2012).

[169] S. Taheri. The link between short sleep duration and obesity: we should recommend more sleep to prevent obesity. *Archives of Disease in Childhood, 91*:881-884. (2006).

[170] E. M. Wickwire, et al. Patient-reported benefits from the pre-sleep routine approach to treating insomnia: Findings from a treatment development trial. *Sleep and Biological Rhythms, 7*:71-77. (2009).

[171] M. Thorpy. Sleep hygiene. Accessed on January 1, 2013 at http://www.sleepfoundation.org/article/ask-the-expert/sleep-hygiene. (2003).

[172] Y. Adachi, et al. A brief behavior therapy administered by correspondence improves sleep and sleep-related behavior in poor sleepers. *Sleep and Biological Rhythms, 6:*16-21. (2008).

[173] D. E. Watenpaugh. (2009).

[174] D. T. Puterbaugh. Searching for a good night's sleep: What mental health counselors can do about the epidemic of poor sleep. *Journal of Mental Health Counseling, 33* (4):312-326. (2011).

[175] L. Lack, et al. The treatment of sleep onset insomnia with bright morning light. *Sleep and Biological Rhythms, 5* (3):173-179. (2007).

[176] Adapted from a report of U.S. Surgeon General. Accessed January 1, 2013 at http://www.cdc.gov/nccdphp/sgr/pdf/execsumm.pdf. (1999).

[177] J. A. Berlin and G. A. Colditz. A meta-analysis of physical activity in the prevention of coronary heart disease. *American Journal of Epidemiology, 132:*612-628. (1990).

[178] Y. Oguma, et al. Physical activity and all cause mortality in women: A review of the evidence. *British Journal of Sports Medicine, 36:*162-172. (2002).

[179] S. N. Blair, et al. Changes in physical fitness and all-cause mortality A prospective study of healthy and unhealthy men. *Journal of the American Medical Association, 273:*1093-1098. (1995).

[180] F. J. Apullan, et al. Usefulness of self-reported leisure-time physical activity to predict long-term survival in patients with coronary heart disease. *American Journal of Cardiology, 102* (4):375-379. (2008).

[181] D. Laurin, et al. Physical activity and risk of cognitive impairment and dementia in elderly persons. *Archives of Neurology, 58:*498-504. (2001).

[182] N. Mutrie and G. Faulkner. Physical Activity: Positive Psychology in Motion. P. A. Linley and S. Joseph (Eds.) In *Positive Psychology in Practice* (pp. 146-164). Hoboken, New Jersey: John Wiley & Sons, Inc. (2004).

[183] K. Weir. The exercise effect. *Monitor on Psychology, 42* (11):48-52. (December, 2011).

[184] H. S. Friedman and L. R. Martin. (2011).

[185] J. A. Halbert, et al. The effectiveness of exercise training in lowering blood pressure: A meta-analysis of randomised controlled trials of 4 weeks or longer. *Journal of Human Hypertension, 11:*641-649. (1997).

[186] N. C. Barengo, et al. Low physical activity as a predictor for total and cardiovascular disease mortality in middle-aged men and women in Finland. *European Heart Journal, 25:*2204-2211. (2004).

[187] C. Boreham and C. Riddoch. The physical activity, fitness and health of children. *Journal of Sports Science, 19:*915-929. (2001).

[188] K. L. Ong, et al. (2007).

[189] A. G. Renehan, et al. Obesity and cancer: Pathophysiological and biological mechanisms. *Archives of Physiology and Biochemistry, 114* (1):71-83. (2008).

[190] A. Novotney. Bite, chew, savor. *Monitor on Psychology, 43* (10):42-45. (November 2012).

[191] L. Winerman. How to eat better—mindlessly. *Monitor on Psychology, 42* (9):46-47. (October 2011).

[192] D. Jakubowicz, et al. Meal timing and composition influence ghrelin levels, appetite scores and weight loss maintenance in overweight and obese adults. *Steroids, 77* (4):323-331. (2012).

[193] A. Kong, et al. Self-Monitoring and Eating-Related Behaviors Are Associated with 12-Month Weight Loss in Postmenopausal Overweight-to-Obese Women. *Journal of the Academy of Nutrition and Dietetics, 112* (9):1428-1435. (2012).

[194] P. N. Mitrou, et al. Mediterranean dietary pattern and prediction of all-cause mortality in a U. S. population: results from the NIH-AARP Diet and Health Study. *Archives of Internal Medicine, 167*:2461-2468. (2007).

[195] C. Féart, et al. Adherence to a Mediterranean diet, cognitive decline, and risk of dementia. *Journal of the American Medical Association, 302* (6):638-648. (2009).

[196] H. Gardener, et al. Mediterranean Diet and White Matter Hyperintensity Volume in the Northern Manhattan Study. *Archives of Neurology, 69* (2):251-256. (2012).

[197] M. L. Daviglus, et al. Fish consumption and the 30-year risk of fatal myocardial infarction. *New England Journal of Medicine, 336* (15):1046-1053. (1997).

[198] National Heart, Lung, and Blood Institute. Disease Statistics, Chapter 4. *Your guide to lowering your blood pressure with DASH.* NIH Publication No. 06-4082. Bethesda, MD: National Institutes of Health. Accessed on December 12, 2012 at http://www.nhlbi.nih.gov/health/public/heart/hbp/dash/new_dash. pdf. (2006).

[199] G. E. Fraser, et al. A possible protective effect of nut consumption on risk of coronary heart disease. The Adventist Health Study. *Archives of Internal Medicine, 152*:1416-1424. (1992).

C. M. Albert, et al. Nut consumption and decreased risk of sudden cardiac death in the physicians' health study. *Archives of Internal Medicine, 162*:1382-1387. (2002).

[200] J. M. Gaziano, et al. A prospective study of consumption of carotenoids in fruits and vegetables and decreased cardiovascular mortality in the elderly. *Annals of Epidemiology, 5*:255-260. (1995).

[201] H. Karpparen and E. Mervaala. Sodium intake and hypertension. *Progress in Cardiovascular Diseases, 49* (2):59-75. (2006).

DON'T LET FEAR

HOLD YOU BACK.

MOVE BEYOND THE PAIN AND
STEP OUT INTO **FREEDOM.**

The author shares details concerning the **emotional and physical symptoms** related to the subject as well as ways to overcome these difficulties.

Readers will find **words of comfort and hope** through Scripture, examples from the Bible of those dealing with difficulties, and practical advice on surviving the difficult situation they are facing.

A **list of resources** is given to encourage further help where needed.

ALSO AVAILABLE from Dr. Moody

randall house
randallhouse.com
(800) 877-7030

d6family.com

Read for yourself ---- Give to a friend

Dr. Moody desires for readers to look holistically at their life and see activities as well as behaviors that can enhance it physically, psychologically, and spiritually, which can lead to major life improvement. He shares research that proves the connection between spiritual health and physical health. The 10 therapeutic life changes are all items that everyone can incorporate into a healthy lifestyle.

Visit **www.FirstAidForYourEmotionalHurts.com**
for more information.

Edward E. Moody Jr. has been a counselor educator at North Carolina Central University since 1995. He is a Professor of Counselor Education, and Chair of the Department of Allied Professions. Moody also serves as pastor at Tippett's Chapel in Clayton, NC. As a minister he has helped people with a variety of difficulties, and as a psychological consultant he has counseled troubled youth. He has a Ph.D. from North Carolina State University in counselor education, an M.A. from Middle Tennessee State University in clinical psychology, and a B.A. from Welch College in pastoral training. He is a Licensed Professional Counselor in NC as well as a Licensed Health Services Provider-Psychological Associate. His first book published was entitled *First Aid for Emotional Hurts – Helping People Through Difficult Times* and has become an excellent resource for ministers. Dr. Moody has also published several articles in scholastic journals and serves as a workshop leader for various events within the Christian community and counseling community. He and his wife, Lynne, live in North Carolina, along with their two children.

Price: $4.99
RELIGION / Christian Ministry / General
ISBN 10: 0-89265-683-2
ISBN 13: 978-0-89265-683-7

randall house
randallhouse.com

9 780892 656837

Illustrations for Bulletin Boards,
Home Bulletins, and News Releases

Clip-Art Features for
Church Newsletters 4

George W. Knight, Compiler
Howard Paris, Illustrator